Selling
Retail

JOHN F. LAWHON

WITH CATHERINE D. LAWHON

J. FRANKLIN, PUBLISHER   TULSA, OKLAHOMA

BOOK TWO

BOOK TWO

SELLING RETAIL: NOW!

IV.

V.

NOW!

NOW THE SELLING BEGINS.
Now is the moment of truth.

You have determined the best product your company has
to solve your customer's problem—and you are going
to sell it to them.

Let the sale begin!

Phase Four: Presenting

THE PRESENTATION

Greeting is not selling.
Qualifying is not selling.
Selecting is not selling.

A ll are critical to the sale and, obviously, if you don't accomplish them, there can be no presentation. **But it is with the presentation that the sale begins.** You know that the benefits your customer gets from your product are the only reason he will buy. You establish the benefits with your presentation.

Greeting, qualifying and selecting are steps you must take in *preparation* for your presentation. The better job you do on each of them the more effective your presentation will be.

When the customer says, "I'll take it," shut up and start writing the order. The sale is made, your job is over — at least that's what selling "experts" would have you believe. By the time you have read and absorbed this book, I hope I have helped you to understand clearly how this response is the last outpost of the loser in professional selling, and why you should know more about selling and closing than I have found is currently being taught in any books or seminars.

If this book has any one great contribution to make to professional retail selling, it is its stress on the importance of buyer awareness of *all* the potential benefits his purchase offers. ◀

The better buy is determined by how much the benefits promised to your customer surpass in value the price asked. Word-of-mouth selling that will ultimately multiply your professional sales and income will come in direct proportion to your customer's excitement and satisfaction. In turn, that

will come in direct proportion to the extent the promised benefits exceed the price paid.

▶ *Please reread that paragraph.*

Oh sure, you can stop pointing out features and benefits the minute the customer says, "I'll take it." Go ahead. Write up the sale and walk the customer out the door with the absolute minimum of excitement and there is no reason for that customer to go out of his way to brag about his new purchase. He gets his approval in direct proportion to the excitement of the buy he made. Whether he paid too much or not will depend on how well you have equipped him with information on the full range of features your product has.

He will buy your product when you get him emotionally involved in the benefits he can expect to enjoy once he owns it, *but after he has bought your product based on those emotions, he'll still have to support his buying decision with logic.*

That decision to buy was based on emotions aroused by the promise of potential benefits through ownership of your product.

His justification for having bought will be based on logic, but the features must support the buying decision after he owns your product.

Greeting, qualifying, selecting are preparation.

PRESENTATION IS SELLING

When I was about nine, I learned my greatest single lesson in selling. The hard way.

Once a month my mother would send me to make the monthly household payments. This was in the mid-1930s when payments were always in cash. She would give me envelopes with money for the gas and electric bill, telephone bill, house payment, and piano payment. I got two trolley tokens and a quarter I could spend at the dime store after my errands were done. I always looked forward to this adventure with great excitement. Back in 1938, a quarter was a fortune and it could keep me occupied for hours in the dime store, trying to decide what to spend it on.

For some unremembered reason, I wound up with an extra dollar of my mother's money on one of those trips.

As I was shopping to spend my quarter, I spotted a pitchman on the main aisle of the dime store behind an elevated counter which was just about eye level to me. He started his patter with, "Ladies and gentlemen, step right this way for a free demonstration of the latest man-made modern miracle-working utensils for your kitchen. You will see for the first time devices that can change some of your most wearisome tasks into exciting experiences. Everybody gather around, step up as close as you can, make room for the folks in the rear."

Before his spiel was well underway, my little nine-year-old chin was planted dead center on that counter.

His first demonstration caused my eyes to bug out. It was a gadget that when spiraled into a carrot, potato, or cucumber would slice it in a corkscrew fashion that left it in a single piece that could be stretched out like an accordion or with one tap of a sharp knife, would fall into a row of perfect slices.

What a miracle it was! And I was one of the first people in the state of Oklahoma to see it in actual use! Although it had never been offered to the public, he said, when it went on sale in about two weeks you would find them in the kitchen utensil department of every fine store in town and they would sell for $2.50. With that, he tucked this modern miracle into a small box which had "$2.50" printed in large letters on the end. He then placed the box right in front of my eyes while he proceeded to the next miracle-working device, a utensil that could take the core from an apple almost faster than the eye could follow.

If that wasn't enough to justify its $3 price when the public was finally permitted to buy it, he then performed right before my eyes another miraculous feat. With a twist, he stuck this device into an orange and juice flowed out as if from a faucet, filling a glass.

The demonstration went on until ten different miracle-working gadgets had been demonstrated, put in boxes with large retail prices on the end of each — ranging from $1.75 to $3.25 — and when the last device had been demonstrated, boxed and stacked, the total cost of the ten boxes came to over $25. That would be the price of those ten household miracles when they were finally offered to the public and the man knew that once word leaked out, a stampede would ensue as the public raced to their nearest dealer to get these wonderful utensils into their homes. As his speech continued, he quietly placed nine more stacks of the ten items on the counter, making ten stacks in all.

When they were all neatly arranged, he said that in order to spread the word, he was going to sell ten and only ten of these complete sets, knowing that just to see them operating friends and neighbors would come from near and far, and through the placement of only ten sets in Oklahoma City, the demand would become so great stores wouldn't be able to keep them in stock.

As he continued, he was whisking each of the ten stacks into a paper bag. As the last stack disappeared, he said, "Now here is the most amazing part of this offer." The ten sets would be sold to the first ten people who laid $1 on that counter. All $25-plus in merchandise would go to the first ten people lucky enough to get their dollar down and no more would be offered at less than the regular prices, which would total over $25.

Needless to say, my mother's dollar was the first one on the counter, and before the tenth bill hit the counter, I was racing for the trolley to show her what a fantastic buy I had made.

My emotions were racing in a hundred different directions. Completely out of breath, I found a seat on the trolley and as I rode along, full of elation, I looked at the prices on the end of the boxes in my bag. To this day, I can see them in technicolor — $2.50, $2.75, $3.00, $3.00, $3.25, $1.75, $2.25, $2.00, $2.00, $2.25 — as I shook the bag to catch a glimpse of each price. $25.25 and I had bought it all for only one of my mother's dollars!

What a deal I had made for her. As I rode along, I couldn't resist breaking open the box that contained the corkscrew knife he had demonstrated first. I just had to have one more look at it.

When I got it out, my heart took a little dip.

It was in fact nothing but a piece of tin can cut into a strip one-half inch by two inches with a wood screw through each end. Obviously this was not the razor sharp device that had so miraculously made an accordion of that carrot, potato, and cucumber.

Well, I consoled myself, maybe that one isn't all he said it was. But I still have nine other gadgets worth a fortune in themselves.

As the trolley wobbled along, a nagging doubt began to overtake me. With much trepidation, I opened the second box, the orange juicer and apple corer. It too was a piece of a coffee can — with the printing still on it! It was cut on the ends by pinking shears and bent into an one-inch tube.

My fears became panic as the full extent of the fraud became apparent. I opened box after box, finally realizing with dread that I had wasted an entire dollar bill that belonged to my family. I was petrified and frantic. I sneaked home and hid behind the garage until it was almost dark and my parents were becoming alarmed at my not having returned from town.

Finally, I came in and confessed to the horrible thing I had done. The experience was so traumatic that as I write about it today I still feel the same emotions, as if the incident had happened only moments ago.

So that was it — my first realization that everyone buys with emotion and justifies with logic.

I bought with emotion. Later, as I examined each item and realized that it was a fraud, I knew I had been taken. That, my friend, to a greater or lesser degree, is what happens every time a sale is made.

Had the products been as represented, with values of $25.25 that would give the miraculous benefits I had been promised, my story would have had an entirely different ending. My family and I would be retelling it to this day. As it happened, it was my last visit to that dime store and to this day, some 47 years later, I still get depressed if I have to visit an old-fashioned dime store.

I wish I could teach every student of selling this lesson as vividly as I learned it for only one of their family's dollars, but alas, the best I can hope for is that you can learn from my embarrassing testimony.

> **Your customer will buy emotionally and he will justify that buying decision with logic after he owns your product.**

> **Features presented in a demonstration logically support that decision once a customer owns your product.**

> **The more features, the more benefits, the more emotion.**

> **The more features, the more logic is added to reinforce that buying decision.**

Whenever I hear "As soon as the customer says 'I will take it,' just shut up and start writing. The sale is made," I can't help but cringe as I remember how I prayed that those gadgets might somehow contain the quality features I needed to support logically my emotional buying decision, so I could have the approval of all those whose approval was important to me. My dismal failure to get it has scarred indelibly my brain and caused H. L. Green's Dime Store to live always in infamy in my mind.

Each of you, if you will try to recall the buying mistakes you have made, can relate to my story. Remember the excitement you experienced when the benefits promised were so great and the price asked was so low? Can you remember when the truth dawned on you? The quality features were not there to assure those benefits and your logic exposed the full extent of your buying error. It was a horrible experience, wasn't it?

Before we proceed, let me assure you that I have made hundreds of buying errors since I was nine. It's just that that one was my most memorable.

> **The salesperson's only job is to give the buyer the information needed to make the best buying decision. It is as much a fraud to cheat the buyer out of needed information as it is to give him false and misleading information.**

► Remember the 9-Dot Revelation? I learned far more about selling from my boyhood experience because of what was done wrong than I did from what was done right. No question about that. The salesman made a great presentation of benefits that got me emo-
► tionally involved and wanting to enjoy those benefits. No question about the fact that *none* of the promised features existed so of course
► no benefits could be enjoyed. Understanding these two critical points is pivotal for every sales career.

When you understand that the presentation is when you actually start selling, then and only then can you realize the importance of the five groups of knowledge. Salespeople who make the effort to get the five groups of knowledge know they are critical to making the sale.

> **Until you begin your presentation everything you have done has been to determine what you are going to sell. Now, you are going to start selling it.**
>
> **Your objective? Pile up benefits your customer can expect to enjoy once he or she owns your product.**

Only when the value of the benefits exceeds the price of your product is the sale possible. Not before.

You reach that critical point by taking each and every feature of your product and showing your customers the benefits of that feature. The sum total of demonstrated benefits *feature by feature* creates the true value of your product.

BEGIN BY PRESENTING VISIBLE FEATURES

Selling a product at retail is almost like having a script all written out for you, because your product is your script. Look at your product and start pointing out each and every visible feature. That's so easy that you can actually do it with little or no knowledge of the product. It's when you come to concealed features that you have to know the score.

Don't make the mistake of thinking that the visible features are so obvious it would be an insult to the customer's intelligence to point them out.

If you really understand the principle of reflection you know how lethal that oversight can be to a sale. More important, *even if your* ◀ *customers do notice the feature, they don't know the benefits and they only buy for the benefits.*

A second mistake even the best-informed salespeople sometimes make in their sales presentations is to believe their main job is pointing out and demonstrating features that are concealed, which can be just as deadly to the sale. Here's why. The exterior is all that will be seen of the product. The outside appearance is supported when quality is added to the product by the unseen features. We can all agree with that, can't we? But these are still not the reasons your customer is going to buy your product.

He will buy for the benefits he expects to get from features both seen and unseen.

Many features can *be* seen, even though you may have to turn your product upside down or even cut it open to do so. But the benefits your customer expects to derive from seen and unseen features cannot be seen because they are emotional, so, they're not in your script. This is what you must learn. **The ability to describe benefits is a treasure of the truly great salespeople. But the most gifted,** silver-tongued, sweet-talking person in the world is spouting nothing but hot air when he only claims features for his product. You insult your customer's intelligence when all you do is point out features he or she can plainly see.

Many an interview hour was spent listening to weak salespersons saying that they rarely got a customer who was interested in the nuts and bolts of their product. Their customers only wanted to know how much it cost or how much down and how much a month it would cost. Stupid? Yes. Yet I heard that over and over. They even insisted that when customers demanded product knowledge it was because something was wrong with the customers.

Consider how damaging this attitude can be to your career. It leads you to believe that because only a minimum of product knowledge will be used in any sale, that you only *need* a minimum. But, *which bit of knowledge will you need?*

Soil-repellent fabric treatment is a feature with benefits for the customer that are so marvelous almost every woman in the world today is willing to pay an extra $70 to get it added to her new sofa. (If you think knowledge of this feature is unimportant in selling, if you feel that demonstrating its benefits is unimportant, then selling is not for you.)

The miraculous X-framed refrigerator door and the magnetic door seal offer the customer immeasurable benefits. (If you think knowing about these features is unimportant in selling refrigerators, if you think showing the benefits of these features is unimportant, then selling is not for you.)

Here's another hidden feature that affords marvelous benefits for the customer. Over the years, squeaking springs in sofas and chairs were irritating. Many customers didn't think of that when they were shopping, but, when I showed a customer how springs were attached to the frame by a metal hinge with a nylon bushing, and told them that as long as they had that piece of furniture they would never hear a squeak, the sale was made. (If that benefit sounds trivial to you, then selling is not for you.)

I don't know how many dinette sets I have sold only because I put a chair on the table to demonstrate how the nylon leg glides pivoted to remain flat on the floor if someone leaned back in the chair. At the same time, I always pointed out how the back of the chair was padded, so that if it bumped against the wall, it would not scratch or mar the surface. Floors and walls in dining areas are often scarred by gouges from chairs that don't have this feature. While most dinette sets have this feature to eliminate damaged floors, not one in a thousand so-called salespeople demonstrates it.

To me, the most valuable feature of a sleeper sofa is the fact that with the sleep unit half-way out, a housewife can tilt the entire sofa forward *with one hand* in order to run a vacuum cleaner under it. In hundreds of interviews, the salespeople were seldom even aware of that feature so you can guess how often they demonstrated it.

The losers are right! The customer is not interested in nor excited about the nuts and bolts.

The customer *is* intrigued, excited by the wonderful benefits which will be enjoyed once he or she owns the product. And, it is only for those benefits that the customer will pay money.

No Claim for Your Product Should Be Made Without Immediate Support

In his essay on compensation, Emerson writes, "From he who makes no claim nothing can be taken."

This principle of life is often violated. All lawsuits stem from it — somebody claims something is his and someone else contests it. When you claim anything as yours, someone else can contest your claim and try to take it away from you.

When you say, "This is a beautiful automobile," you have asked the customer to agree with your claim, which is only an opinion. The fact that the customer says yes or no does not mean that she agrees or disagrees with you. Customers are rarely contentious when you make claims for your product or company. When you claim an automobile is beautiful, your customer's reaction may be one of total disbelief. He may have been standing there looking at your car, thinking "That is the ugliest car I have ever seen!" and before he can express his opinion you make your claim.

Frequently, when you make a claim, you have lost the sale.

You may continue with your presentation and the customer is usually polite enough to let you go on, but once you make a claim that is an unsupported opinion with which the customer disagrees silently, your sale is dead in the water. When you get to the close, all the tricky techniques in the world won't get that sale, because the customer simply tunes you out. This is an ideal time to reread "Old Ugly Was a Dog."

To review:

> You are not actually selling until you begin your presentation.

> Only when the customer believes that the benefits of an item exceed its price in value will he or she buy.

> Customers buy with emotion but they must be able to support their buying decisions later with logic.

> Begin your presentation by describing the benefits of visible features, but don't forget the benefits of invisible features.

> Never make a claim that you cannot support immediately and convincingly.

29

Phase Four: Presenting

CUSTOMER INVOLVEMENT

"**M**r. Jones, that coffee table is solid oak. Just pick up the end of it and feel its weight."

"Mrs. Jones, the natural oak finish has been hand-buffed to a satin smoothness. Just rub your hand over that finish. It almost feels like satin, doesn't it?"

"Mrs. Jones, take one finger and open that drawer. Feel how smoothly it glides in and out on the hot-waxed oak center guide. Because the hot wax impregnates the solid oak it will glide as smoothly as that for years and years to come."

Salespeople who sell cars may be the biggest offenders on this one point. Telling a customer how it drives, that it has power windows, seats, or anything else is a waste of time. Let the customer drive it, smell the "new," operate the windows, adjust the seat, and listen to the stereo. That is selling. (One of the best car salesmen I ever met had me observe the turn signal lever and how it shut off on even the slightest turns.)

Once, I was considering a new bass boat. The salesman told me how much smoother it rode in rough water than my present one. I didn't buy it. If he had had the boat ready to hook to a trailer on his car, he could have said "Hop in" and driven three minutes to the city reservoir as he told me about the boat. Then, I could have experienced that smooth ride. That's selling. All he was doing was telling.

Your presentation must utilize each of these opportunities:

1. *Involve every one of the customer's five senses if possible.*

Get him to look at the item by using the Principle of Reflection and pointing out one feature at a time. Getting him to feel it. If it has a fragrance, as in the case of a cedar chest, new car or leather chair,

Now! / 11

get him to smell it. (Nothing smells better than new leather, for example.) If the springs are squeak-free, get him to listen. If there is something to taste, get him to do that. Get as many of his senses involved as you can in your presentation and demonstration. Have the customer drive it, push the button, turn the dial, sink into the seat, lie down on it, walk on it, try it on, use it. Even though they may be clumsy it is still better if they do it themselves.

2. *Get them emotionally involved with your product.*

Help them visualize it in their home, feel its softness, think of how pretty it will be. Use emotion-involving words like love, dream, imagine, hope, happiness, excitement as you get them involved emotionally in your product.

Present visible features first, then invisible ones, making every effort to demonstrate hidden features. Turn it upside down so the customer can see the features as you describe specific benefits he will enjoy.

Never mention a feature without supporting it with at least two benefits that the customer will receive when he owns that product with that feature, thus establishing that other similar products without that feature may not provide those benefits.

Demonstrate every feature that can be demonstrated and get the customer to participate in your demonstration to the fullest extent possible. Make your presentations dramatic.

Talk about owning the product, not about buying it. Customers love to own. When you have them thinking of how it would be to own your product, you are very close to a sale. But always get the customer's opinion first, then support it.

Remember one thing about your presentation: it is your responsibility to make the customer aware of every feature and benefit that your product has to offer, even if a feature or benefit doesn't seem important at the time you are making the sale.

Every one of your presentations will include these major points:

1. Show how your product has overcome or eliminated those features that were undesirable on the customer's old product. "New and improved" is your stock in trade.

2. Make it clear that your product has features the customer said he would like on his new purchase.

3. When a feature meets one of the customer's needs, as determined during the qualifying phase of the sale, make your point thoroughly as you remind the customer of his stated need.

4. Be sure every need the customer posed during qualifying has been met. Show features and give benefits necessary to meet every need. Or, agree on a compromise, wherein the customer agrees to forego his stated product need in favor of features that give more desirable benefits, thus overcoming the needs that are less important to him.

5. Never ignore a customer's genuine stated need during your presentation or you will pay for it in lost sales when you try to close.

6. Use any and all sales tools and materials available to strengthen your presentation.

7. Maintain higher authority support for the status and confidence of your product when possible. (More to come on this subject.)

8. Always point out feature benefits even if they aren't needed to make the sale.

9. Learn to brag about what might be a problem to the customer if he discovered it himself. If no two pieces of wood are alike, for example, explain how uniqueness is a benefit.

10. Create mental images of benefits.

Let's go over each of these in detail:

1. Ever wonder why so many TV commercials say "new and improved?" The main thrust might be for one person to say "I bet my (shampoo, deodorant, toothpaste, mouthwash or whatever) is better than yours." Person A argues, "Mine is the best because I use brand XYZ," then Person B crows, "So do I, but mine is new and improved XYZ."

If you were the maker of brand XYZ and you already had a major share of your market, how would you get new customers? How would you get back former customers who had used your product, liked it, but had been wooed away by another brand? How would you strengthen the confidence in your brand in people already happily using it to insulate them from susceptibility to other brand claims?

Add the words "new and improved" to your advertising claim!

To the person who has almost tried your product but not quite been won over, "new and improved" says "Hey, if you thought about us before, think again. There is even more reason to try us now. We were the best, but now we are even better."

To your loyal user it says "You were so happy with our product that we want you to know you can be even happier because now we are better."

The real hook — and the one most people miss — is this: "If you were once our loyal customer and for some reason were wooed away to another brand that you've found isn't any better than our old one, come on back, because we've made our product far superior. Sure we felt it was the best before, but now it is even better. Now it is new and improved."

Let's see how these magic words can work in your presentation.

> CUSTOMER: I don't want foam rubber cushions because my last sofa had foam rubber cushions and they gave off a terrible odor.
>
> SALESPERSON: Mrs. Jones, did you like the comfort and durability of foam rubber and how well it held its shape, never getting lumpy?
>
> CUSTOMER: Sure, the comfort and durability were great, but because of that odor, I have been hoping for ten years now that they would wear out so I could get rid of the odor and get a new sofa. You'll never sell me foam rubber again.
>
> SALESPERSON: Mrs. Jones, I have some exciting news for you. Since you bought your old sofa, science has developed a new foam for cushions that is so improved it is odorless when they make it and they guarantee it to remain that way as long as you have it.
>
> This new foam gives you seating comfort superior to foam rubber. It holds its shape better and longer than the

finest foam rubber. Plus, they have developed a synthetic fiber which when made into fluffy layers and wrapped around this foam, makes it feel just like the most luxurious and expensive goose down.

And one other thing, Mrs. Jones, every particle of the filling in the cushion is now absolutely allergy-free. Mrs. Jones, these new cushions are such an improvement over any other type of cushion you can buy today that you are going to find it hard to believe. The material is nylon, too. Come on over here and sit on one. I want you to experience this new and improved cushion.

When the first nylon carpet was introduced, it created so much static electricity that they had to weave copper wires into the back and ground them to a building's plumbing. Even then, the static electricity was so severe that it could actually burn you. But after several years of new and improved static arrestors, nylon carpet is almost static free.

Early nylon yarn was a spun fiber created almost the same way cotton candy is. It was so unstable that the fibers in the yarn would roll up into hard balls wherever there was a lot of traffic. These balls were so big and so hard they had to be cut out of the carpet with a razor blade. Continuous filament processes eliminated that "pilling" effect. Nylon fiber has been made in new and improved ways almost yearly since it was first discovered. Today's nylon fibers are far superior to those early products.

Nylon fiber is non-porous, so dye could not penetrate the fibers in early nylon carpets. After a year or two of use the color began to rub off, leaving blotched patches that looked bad to say the least. A later development mixed colors right into the nylon solution while it was a liquid, producing the most color-fast fiber ever developed. Since then, *new* and *improved* dyeing processes for all fibers have been developed.

In this computer age the technical breakthroughs have come so fast that by the time a new computer is introduced, produced, and delivered to the first user, a new and improved model has already made the first one obsolete. Each new and improved computer has brought the price down in equally dramatic fashion.

Technology develops at such a frenzied pace that any product available today contains hosts of new and improved features that promise brand new benefits to your customer. How exciting it is to be a part of this generation and to be the person chosen to tell customers about all of the exciting new and improved features that can give benefits never before available! **Yes, your customer can be not only the first kid on the block to enjoy the benefits of those features. Sometimes they can even be the first kid in history to do so.**

You can make that excitement a part of your life if you learn everything there is to know about your product and keep up-to-date on the "new and improved." Imagine how anxious you'll be to find out what your customers didn't like about their last products now that you know these problems have been eliminated by your new and improved product.

2. *Most of the time, what a customer did not like about his last product and the changes or additions he would like in his new product are one and the same thing.* Besides new and improved features, there are many, many technical developments in products today that were never available in the old ones, permitting you to show a new product with added features promising even greater benefits.

Take the new recliner chairs. In the past few years some marvelous features have been added to them. Probably the most dramatic is a glide-out feature, originated by Berkline and adapted and developed by all quality manufacturers, that actually moves the entire chair forward as it reclines. This mechanism's importance to the customer is that it permits a reclining chair to be placed against the wall of the room, saving as much as 12 inches of room space over some earlier models. Bases that swivel 360 degrees are available, too. And, you can now buy well-styled chairs that rock, recline, swivel and glide out from the wall automatically, offering versatility and comfort unsurpassed by older chairs at prices that are really quite modest.

Because there are so many new features on recliners today, every customer you wait on is a prospect. He doesn't have to wait until his old item is worn out if new and improved ones have come out.

> **Think about how many times a car changes hands before it is worn out. Don't think of the customer who bought the used car, think of the person who sold it long before it was worn out. He sold that**

perfectly good automobile because he had been offered a new and improved model.

3. When you reach your presentation phase, you realize how important it is to make notes of the things the product can do for the customer, and the benefits he would like to enjoy when he owns a new product, i.e. the information you obtained as you qualified the customer's needs.

As you make your presentation, you know what the product must do for the customer. As you show and demonstrate each feature be sure you get the customer emotionally involved in the benefit so that he experiences it fully with his senses. Those promised benefits must be experienced *mentally* by your customers, too.

4. As each need (determined while qualifying) is met, be sure the customer is satisfied that this product will fully meet that need. Don't just gloss over or hurry through any feature benefit or combination of feature benefits that meets an expressed need of the customer. Be sure you have satisfied the customer on each point.

5. If a customer needs a desk with a file drawer and the desk the customer saw, wants, and can't live without doesn't have a file drawer, recommend a separate file. The file drawer was only one of a dozen reasons the customer needed the desk.

In today's world, your customer needs more than one file drawer anyway. A perfect solution lies in the storage files sold at office supply companies. Remember everyone's required to keep tax records for seven years. You can buy a new drawer each year for about $10 and at the end of the year simply date the drawer and store it, so an entire year's records are available (and in order) any time you need them.

You get the idea. **Your product may be perfect for your customer, but still leave an important need unmet. You must satisfy that customer's need or you may not make the sale. It is up to you to think "outside the 9-dots," figure out a solution and offer it to the customer.**

How many times have you fallen in love with a very expensive dress or found a really good-looking sport coat, and the commissioned salesperson sent you off to some other department to search for the shoes, purse, belt, or other accessories to go with your purchase? If you fail to find it, you may leave without buying anything.

The responsible, professional salesperson makes sure you have a satisfactory solution to all of your needs just as in the case of the desk customer:

> SALESPERSON: Mrs. Jones, do you have an office supply store you are presently using?
>
> CUSTOMER: No.
>
> SALESPERSON: Let me get the Yellow Pages and find one near you.

Whereupon the salesperson hurries to the office, looks in the Yellow Pages, locates an office supply store close to customer's home, calls it, gets the price of storage file drawers, and returns to the customer in less than three minutes, handing her a slip of paper.

> SALESPERSON: Mrs. Jones, here is the address of XYZ Office Supply. I called and they have the storage drawers we talked about and the price is only $8.95. That would solve your filing needs, wouldn't it?

This need has been met and will not come up when you start to close, dealing your sale a death blow. Later on, you will encounter this subject again, as you read the chapter entitled "Service Beyond the Call of Duty."

6. *Use sales aids when making presentations and be sure they are kept fresh and new-looking.*

If you show a customer an old, dog-eared card, sign, pamphlet, magazine, cutaway sample, fabric swatch, or any other sales aid, you are by association showing her what her new furniture will soon look like. I didn't say don't use sales aids; I said don't use scruffy, dirty ones.

Used properly, good sales aids can make you a lot of sales and a lot of money, so take advantage of every one you can get your hands on. Insist on new and fresh sales aids whenever yours start to get a little ratty.

If you stop using them, the factories will stop supplying them.

Nothing you can say about a coil spring will get your message across like showing the customer a coil spring and letting him feel it for himself.

Nothing you can say about a double-dowelled wood joint with

corner blocks that are glued and screwed into place will ever really make a lady understand their true value. When you show her a cutaway, however, your point is made. You reveal superior quality promising far greater durability and the peace of mind that comes from knowing the kids aren't going to break it down.

No bedding department should ever be without cutaway samples of the complete line of mattresses and box springs. When your competitor could not or would not show the customer what was inside his mattress, she may have thought that it was because he had something to hide. *When you voluntarily expose every concealed feature of your product, the customer's confidence level shoots straight up.*

Get you hands on every good sales tool you can find and use it.

Once, years ago, I carried a line of fine Early American furniture that featured a catalytic varnish finish. I became their biggest dealer. My secret?

That finish was so hard that even fingernail polish remover would not damage it. I kept on hand cases of polish remover in sample-size bottles. We'd demonstrate the finish by making an "X" in red fingernail polish on our most expensive pieces. A customer would always say, "My goodness, how could you ever do a terrible thing like that to such a beautiful piece of furniture?" Whereupon the salesperson would whip out a rag and polish remover and with a whisk the polish came off, leaving the expensive finish undamaged.

Then the salesperson would explain that we did it to demonstrate our finish. When you bought furniture of this quality, you expected to use it for a lifetime, and chances are very good that over the years, something like polish remover, alcohol, nail polish, or a thousand other things around your home would be spilled on the finish, any one of which if spilled on other good and equally expensive finishes would eat right through the finish to the wood.

Then we gave them a free bottle of fingernail polish remover, telling them if they found furniture they liked as well or better, before they bought it they should ask the salesperson if he would let them pour fingernail polish remover on its finish. If he wouldn't, we suggested they come back and buy ours.

A little aside to this story. Over the years, every so often a customer who returned to buy that furniture from us would tell how an unknowing salesperson had said to them "Our finish is as good or better than theirs. If they will let you pour fingernail polish remover on it, so will we." And then learned a terribly expensive lesson.

One more time: When used properly, good sales tools can make you a lot of sales and a lot of money.

Reread the revelation on benefits noting the ScotchGard® and Teflon® stories and what happened when the salespeople quit using sales aids to demonstrate the benefits. Hundreds and hundreds of millions of dollars in sales were lost that could and should have been made with the proper use of sales aids and demonstrations. No true professional ever passes up the opportunity to use good sales tools in his demonstration.

7. *Maintain a good file of higher authority to use when customer confidence needs reinforcing.*

In Tulsa, one of our prominent citizens is Oral Roberts whose healing ministry is known world-wide. I am sure he won't take offense at this humorous story I once heard.

The story goes that when Oral died and arrived at the Pearly Gates, there was a motorcycle escort that raced him through the golden streets of heaven right straight into the presence of God. Whereupon God came down off his throne, rushed up to Oral, and said, "I thought you never would get here." Oral said, "Why, what's the matter?" And God said, "Well, you see, Oral, I have this pain in my back."

Shortly after I heard this story, Oral's lovely wife came into our store to buy a new Posturpedic mattress because their old one was giving Oral a backache. Well, the salesman who sold Mrs. Roberts that sleep set never missed an opportunity when dealing with a prospective bedding customer to pull out his copy of the sales order and say: "You see, folks, when Oral Roberts was having a problem with his back, he bought this sleep set from me." That salesman's bedding sales increased dramatically after he started using Oral Roberts as a higher authority. When you think about it, if Oral Roberts is not a higher authority, I don't know who is. No pun intended, of course.

But the real impact of this sales technique is not a joke. In fact, those professionals who really cash in on it take home thousands of extra dollars every year and they find their sales are made more quickly.

Several years ago, I employed a woman who was a sales leader. She had made a very large sale to a man who was head of our largest competitor's service department and his wife, a top salesperson at another large furniture store. You can bet that saleswoman used that order form every time anyone ever questioned our company's prices or quality.

In Nashville, our store furnished the homes of some of the top country entertainers. In many cases, these fine people have become some of the most famous and revered in America. Occasionally, a fan magazine would feature one of them at home with some furniture from our store clearly shown. The top salespeople always carried those pictures with them.

If you're reading a magazine and you see one of the products you sell pictured with a famous person or shown as having won some design award, cut the page out and keep it between clear plastic sheets so it will stay fresh. When your customer is considering that item, bring out your picture and you will be delighted by how much confidence it will give the customer in his buying decision.

When you have sold an item to very important or well-known people, tell them how excited you were to wait on them and how anxious you are to tell everyone they bought from you. V.I.P.s welcome recognition and adulation regardless of what they say and you are free to use your testimony of their buying decision to help you in future sales. Keep a fresh copy of the sales ticket with their signatures at all times.

One word of warning: Never fake it. Name dropping is the kiss of death and is only practiced by braggarts. Bragging is the surest customer turnoff I know of.

Recently I saw an ad in the *Wall Street Journal* for a used 1980 450 SLC Mercedes coupe, a car that cost around $35,000 when new. The ad said bids would be accepted until a certain day, and then the car would be sold to the highest bidder. The ad stated the terms of the offer: The first minimum bid would be $400,000. That for a used car whose exact duplicate you could buy for $30,000, in many cases with fewer miles and in better condition. Why would anyone pay such a sizable sum for such a car?

For one reason only — the car's previous owner had been Princess Grace of Monaco. Perhaps an auto museum owner or a Hollywood museum owner would buy it to increase their business, because people will pay just to see the cars of famous people. Cars of famous people often bring astronomical prices. To those who own cars exactly like the cars of celebrities, there is status attached. They will enjoy telling anyone who will listen that their car is the same model and year as so-and-so's car which sold at auction for several hundred thousand dollars.

There is the same emotional tie when you can tell your customer that a prominent or famous person has purchased the same item they are considering.

To show you how powerful this can be, Pepsi Cola Company reportedly paid rock star Michael Jackson $7 million to do Pepsi commercials. If Pepsi is willing to pay Michael Jackson $7 million to do a commercial and then another $40 million to buy the time to get it on the air, it's because they know that hundreds of millions of dollars in sales will result.

Don't ever pass up this opportunity when you have an endorsement by somebody famous. Corny as it may seem, the same human trait that makes such persons respected, recognized, and idolized can add enormous value to your product when someone famous owns one too.

In small-ticket retail selling, it is difficult to use this sales tool to the degree that salespeople can who deal in really big-ticket items, but when it comes to selling million-dollar machines, million-dollar construction projects, million-dollar aircraft — the top professionals solicit and use for endorsement every notable customer they can get. Letters from these satisfied users and owners are often their strongest selling tool.

One of the finest motor cars in the world was once the Packard and its manufacturer had one of the greatest sales slogans ever developed for selling cars — "Ask the man who owns one."

Billions of dollars worth of products and services are sold every year with third-party endorsement.

8. *When your product has features and benefits which are not pertinent or necessary to make the sale, they should still be demonstrated anyway, because when your customer buys your product, those features and their benefits go with it,* and in fact are a bonus to that customer. Many times the customer hasn't even thought of a need for those other features, but when you have explained the benefits they can bring him, your product has added value and closing the sale is easier.

I won a national advertising award years ago for a full-color ad I produced for a chair and ottoman. Prize-winning ads are judged by advertising people, and seldom is one of the judging criteria how much the ad *sold*. But, this ad was one of my all-time most successful chair ads.

Here is why I'm telling you about this experience. When I ordered the chairs, I had never seen them. They were a new Danish modern design, which was very big at the time. Because the ad had to be made up nine weeks in advance and went to press five weeks before it appeared in the newspaper, I had to work from the factory's color picture and the copy information they supplied.

The ad was already printed and on its way to the newspaper when a carload of the chairs arrived and I got my first look at them. They looked great — even better than the picture — and they swiveled on ball bearing rollers just as I had said in the ad. But they also rocked. They were swivel rockers. This feature, which the ad said nothing about, changed the value of that chair.

My ad had asked people who wanted and needed only a Danish modern lounge chair and ottoman to come and buy. When they came in, we pointed out a feature and benefits they had not considered before.

It worked like magic. When they found out that for the same advertised price the chair also included a rocking base, they literally snatched them away from us. We had expected that ad to sell a carload, but we wound up selling more than five carloads and many of the buyers had to wait as long as three months for delivery. They were glad to do it when they found out about the benefits of the extra free feature they were getting.

9. You'll learn some very peculiar things about people if you stay long enough in sales. It is people who make sales the exciting profession that it is. Because God never created two individuals exactly alike, your life in sales will never be boring or routine. *To the successful salesperson, this constantly-changing flow of personalities is a big bonus.*

It always amazes me how many sales are lost on delivery (and how much cost is incurred by companies) because the salesperson did not make the customer aware of the true benefits of his product. Typical would be the customer who buys a set of occasional tables in solid wood or with veneer tops and refuses them upon delivery because the pattern in the grain of the wood does not match. Most companies would react to that by exchanging the tables until every table in their stock has been refused by the customer and a refund is made. Even after all that expense and effort, the sale is still lost.

The tragedy of these losses is that the most important and most visible feature of woodcrafted furniture — the variety of the grain —

was never presented to the customer. Therefore, the customer saw the feature as a negative and canceled the order.

Americans are people of the land. We have a love affair with wood. Although many new materials have been introduced in furniture construction, American buyers have spurned them. There is a security, a natural beauty, a warmth, and a hominess, if you will, in wood that we demand in our furniture. No matter how much a part of the space age our homes become, no matter how much steel and plastic we accept in construction of appliances, toys, and vehicles, when it comes to the security and comfort of our homes, we want wood. It is our inheritance as people of the land.

Wood is the only material used in furniture that gives us something that is ours and ours alone, because the beauty of all wood is in the patterns produced by the grain. No two pieces of wood have the same pattern. Any wood furniture you own is unique.

The finish is the most expensive process in fine wood furniture. While almost everything else is automated, most steps in the finishing process of furniture are still performed by craftsmen, whose most important job is to highlight the most beautiful and distinctive part of the wood — the patterns formed by the grain. (Even finishes on popularly priced furniture can still involve as many as 17 steps in the finishing process, to enhance the natural beauty of the wood.)

To this day, one of the most expensive is a fumed finish. Originally, it was achieved by packing the wood in fresh manure whose chemicals emitted fumes that entered the soft, pithy summer growth of the wood, opening the pores even more so stain could penetrate deeply into the surface of the grain. Then the wood could be stained in colors and finished to a soft satin surface that allowed all the natural beauty of the grain to be seen clearly.

The most romantic, the most unusual, the most natural, the most secure, and the most wanted single thing Americans demand in their furniture today is wood and the only way to tell the real thing from the facsimile is that no two pieces are ever alike.

To me, no artist ever painted a picture that approached the beauty of the many different shapes, designs, and characters of the patterns formed by wood grain.

Even the smallest piece of wood can evoke more emotion when its struggles for growth have painted a graphic masterpiece of beauty never to be repeated. When you have learned to love wood, you will have a romance in your presentation that exudes positive, exciting emotion. Then you can get your customer emotionally involved in wood unlike any other material used in your product. It should become the bulwark of your presentation.

No highlight of wood's grain, no defect that makes it the only piece of its kind, should ever be overlooked as you describe its beauty, charm, and romance.

I have gone into great detail about wood for one reason: if there is any art to selling it is at this point. Get your customer involved emotionally in the benefits of your product. There is no question that wood can evoke more emotion than many other things you may be selling. Try it.

Failure at this phase of the sale is one reason why 75% of the salespeople account for only 25% of the sales.

The power of emotion applies no matter what your product. Ray Kroc of McDonald's got excited when he talked about hamburger buns and a paper company owner I once heard got his listeners emotional about toilet paper. But unless you know and love your product, you'll never make that emotion happen. Getting the customer emotionally involved in your product is such a critical part of any sale I want to give you a few more examples.

For years, furniture has had casters on it to make it easier to move. Not long ago, a new caster came on the market that was so superior to all others that even though it was far more expensive, it soon had a corner on the caster business. Today, there are cheap, inferior copies, but the Shepherd caster is still not only remarkably superior in rolling and turning action, but also extremely handsome, adding to the beauty and quality of the furniture. This marvelous feature costs several times the price of cheap plastic copies that have to be replaced constantly.

Now, here comes a possible downfall of this wonderful feature. I doubt if in one out of a thousand cases are the genuine Shepherd casters called to the customer's attention when they are present on furniture sold today. The customer never gets to enjoy the pride of knowing what a truly fine caster she has on her furniture. She can only assume that hers is no better than furniture using cheap copies.

Even worse, Shepherd casters are always shipped with an opaque plastic ring around them for protection. This is supposed to be removed and thrown away when the furniture is delivered into the home. It serves no other purpose. If not removed, soon it will come off anyway. Invariably, that's when the customer comes in, demanding a replacement for his broken caster.

Many times, just as with the occasional tables whose grain doesn't match, no amount of explaining will make that customer believe the plastic ring was not a permanent part of the Shepherd caster. All too often the sale is lost in this manner, or an irate customer is lost to that company forever.

When I read books on selling that say once the customer says "I'll take it," shut up and write up the sale, I think of the billions of dollars wasted on lost sales and expensive service calls because of order takers out to get the money with no regard for customer or company.

When I sold carpet, one of the ways I could see and feel its quality was by the density and depth of its nap. All too often, the customer would remark that thick, lush carpet showed every footprint. In other words, the customer saw the real luxury and beauty of the carpet as a negative. Diplomatically, I would explain that that was the way everyone determined what a really rich and luxurious carpet they had. Once I had convinced the customer of the positives and eliminated the negatives, then, and only then, could the sale of that particular carpet be made.

In the 40s and 50s a big selling item was Deltox rugs. These were good-looking, hard-wearing rugs that were very inexpensive. They were made of craft cord which was actually just twisted paper. After dyeing and weaving, the cords were coated with plastic, which permitted the rugs to be damp mopped.

One day, a lady was brought to me who had asked to see the manager. "What can I do for you?" I asked.

"I want you to come outside and see my Deltox rug," she replied.

When we got to her station wagon, in the back was a wash tub filled with soggy gray pulp.

"Is that your Deltox rug?"

"No, just part of it," she said, "the rest is stuck in my sewer and my automatic washer, where a plumber is trying to get it out."

"Ma'am, surely you didn't put your Deltox rug in your automatic washer, did you?"

"Your salesman told me I could wash it with a garden hose and not damage it," she replied, "so I figured my washer wouldn't hurt it."

When I had refunded her money and paid the plumber's bill, it had cost my company several times the original sale price of the rug. A wonderful, inexpensive rug enjoyed in millions of homes was turned into a nightmare by exaggerating its features. That salesperson lost his commission and his job. No company then or now can afford to do business that way. **Successful selling is above all honest — anything less is not real selling.**

Every salesperson puts his reputation on the line with each presentation. Greeting, qualifying, and selecting are all a matter of technique and expertise, but the presentation involves your basic integrity. Some call the presentation the selling of the product and in truth that is what it is.

By now, it must have occurred to you that *little or none of your presentation can be accomplished effectively without a complete and thorough knowledge of your product, what it does and how it works.*

Here is where most salespeople falter in their attempts to become professionals. They develop a glib and polished approach that gains the customer's confidence. They even become very adept at qualifying the customer's problem. They can become masters in the art of selecting the product for the customer, and the really good ones learn all the little trick closing techniques.

I listen to every sales training tape I can get my hands on, and because so much of this is done in my car, I have a family that has probably been exposed to more sales training than any other in history.

Recently on a long drive from Hot Springs, Arkansas, to Tulsa after several hours of sales tapes on closing the sale, Carey, who was 11 years old said, "Dad, those people all sound tricky and sneaky." Amanda, who was nine, said, "That's all they are, Dad. I sure hope you don't sell that way." I asked what they meant. Their response was: "Dad, all they talk about is ways to trick you into saying you will buy something and ways to get you to sign contracts without you finding out what you are buying or what you are signing."

I have thought about what my children perceived as the essence of sales training that is almost universal and it became apparent that the real heart of selling was being avoided like the plague. The books and tapes tell you that you must master the techniques of selling to enjoy the highest-paying hard work there is and that is absolutely true. But it's not selling if you follow their teaching. You might be well paid, but the work is made harder because it lacks integrity.

The salesperson's job is to supply the information needed for the buyer to make the best buying decision. The techniques are needed only for those non-selling phases.

The only reason the sales close is considered the most important part of the sale by most teachers and writers on sales techniques, is that when little or no selling has taken place, no sale will result unless you can develop — as my daughters put it, "sneaky and tricky ways" to get the prospective buyer to buy. You have not been able to give him the information he needs to make the best buying decision because you did not have that information yourself.

There is no doubt that with the dozens (as some teachers advocate) or hundreds of closes you can use on your unsold customers, you are going to get more orders. *But that approach has nothing to do with selling!* It's nothing more or less than teaching the order taker to be sneaky and tricky in order to coerce the customer into buying. When that is done in the name of selling, no wonder the teachers and practitioners want to hide under a different label such as "marketers" and don't want to take credit for having made a sale honorably.

They prefer to say, "I got that customer happily involved in my product or service."

Of course, they don't want the terms of their sneaky contracts exposed to the bright light of day. They don't want the truth to show. They don't call a down payment a down payment, a monthly payment a monthly payment, or a contract a contract. Everyone knows they are the "initial investment," the "monthly investments," and the "paperwork."

To me, high-pressure salesmen are to be avoided. So is the insidious perpetrator of fraudulent tactics who used them to get an order without having done his job.

> **Your job as salesperson is to provide the information your customer needs to make the best buying decision. If you don't have that information, you are not going to make sales. If someone does buy from you, it was because you took his order or, as many sales manuals advocate, you simply tricked him into saying yes.**

In neither case do you have the right to call yourself a salesperson, because you have stolen the most valuable thing your customer has. You have robbed the customer of his or her time. And if the customer does not receive all of the benefits you implied or falsely promised for your product, that makes you a thief of his or her money, too.

The facts are irrefutable. Without sure knowledge of your (and your competitor's) product, inventory, current advertising, finance plan, and company policies, you are not and never will qualify as a professional salesperson. Without this knowledge, it is impossible to do what you are required to do.

If you don't have all your information, of course you must grasp at any straw in order to close the sale. But with all your information, you are in control. Confident, you make your presentation with the excitement that gets the customer emotionally involved in your product, and the sale is the end result just as naturally as breathing, without your ever being sneaky or tricky.

The true closing is a thrill and a satisfaction only qualified professionals ever experience, but when you experience it one time, you will know at once why selling is the easiest high-paid work there is.

A quick review of the presentation and its objectives:

1. **Your product is your script. Start by pointing out visible features, then proceed to invisible features.**
2. **Present at least two benefits for every feature.**
3. **Demonstrate every feature, even if you think the customer already knows about it, even if the customer doesn't need its benefits immediately.**
4. **Involve your customer emotionally by involving his five senses.**
5. **Use every sales aid you can come up with. Be sure they are clean inside and out.**
6. **Know your product — and your competitors' — inside and out.**
7. **Sum up your presentation by reviewing every customer need and every product feature and how they match up.**

Things you never, never do in your demonstration:

1. **Never knock one of your other products. Every**

product your company carries is the best at its price.

2. Never knock your competitor or his product.
3. Do not talk about yourself.
4. Do not argue with or directly contradict a customer.
5. Never predetermine or give an opinion about what you like or don't like regarding the aesthetic values of a product.
6. Never make a presentation until you have qualified the customer's problem.
7. Never smoke or use even the mildest of foul language, and certainly no curse words — not even damn — in the customer's presence.
8. Never, never, never go forward with a presentation unless you have positive communication with the customer.
9. Never discuss religion or politics with the customer.

Do these things and you're on your way to *enjoying* the easiest high-paid work there is: Professional retail selling!

Always remember one thing *before* you walk your customer out the door without a sale: No matter how hard you worked, or how close you got, your company will not pay you for sales you *almost* make.

Think before you let the customer go. Was there *one* more benefit you could have demonstrated?

Phase Four: Presenting

THE ART OF QUESTIONING

THE KEY TO SELLING

By now, it should be apparent to you that questioning is the key ingredient in selling. Remember the card trick? You asked questions that led a person to choose the card that you wanted him to.

Questioning has come up again and again, but at this point, I feel it is important to isolate certain facets of the subject so you can make a thorough study of them.

The most important single question in every salesperson's vocabulary is: Why?

This word should be a reflex anytime the customer asks a question or makes a statement leaving you cornered or up a blind alley or that you must answer with a no. Your automatic reaction should be "Do you mind if I ask you why?" A few examples follow:

CUSTOMER: I don't like that.

SALESPERSON: I am sure you have a good reason for feeling that way but do you mind if I ask you why?

CUSTOMER: I need it in blue.

SALESPERSON: May I ask you why you need blue?

CUSTOMER: Do you have a 40-cubic-foot refrigerator?

SALESPERSON: That would be a huge refrigerator.
Do you mind if I ask why you need one so large?

Such examples could continue endlessly for any retail situation. With these questions you open up every sale. When you're silent in response to a customer's "I don't like that," you have no place to go and chances are because you don't know why she didn't like that item, you will continue to show her more and more items she doesn't like. But if you ask why she doesn't like it, many times her answer helps clear up her own misunderstanding of the item as well as giving you a clue as to what to show her.

When a customer's request is for a specific item that you don't stock, and your answer is "We don't carry that," no sale will happen. When you ask why she wanted or needed that specific item, you open up the sale. Ask "Why?" when you hear "I want to think about it" or "I will talk it over with my husband."

The second basic facet of questioning is to get customer agreement as you progress in a sale.

During qualifying, your customer says that one of the things she doesn't like about her old sofa is how the legs have always been loose and wobbly. You tip the sofa you have selected for her and you point out how the legs are an extension of the frame and can never come loose and then maybe show her a diagram or cutaway, winding up by saying, "That should solve any loose leg problems. Don't you agree, Mrs. Jones?"

Once you've completed your presentation of a product that had none of the undesirable things she mentioned but actually had more features and benefits than she had expected and she has agreed that each feature was, in fact, all she wanted and more, then closing the sale is an accomplished fact as all great salespeople will attest.

Some sample questions:

This is the perfect length, isn't it?

It does have all of the comfort you want, doesn't it?

It will be good to know that your children can't open the car door or fall out once you have pushed this safety button that locks all the doors of the car, won't it?

Because the fabric is 100% Dupont nylon, you can expect it to wear like iron, can't you?

You did say that this was the color you wanted, didn't you?

It's nice to know that it's guaranteed for five years, wouldn't you agree?

It should solve that problem, shouldn't it?

This one piece by itself wouldn't meet your needs, would it?

Your entire family can sit comfortably at this table and the extra leaves would let you seat up to six extra guests on special occasions, don't you agree?

I can get it delivered to you on Thursday, and that's perfect, isn't it?

You can buy it with 10% down and spread the payments over 48 months. We agreed that is within your budget, didn't we?

Without further examples, you should be able to see that while no one of these agreements from the customer actually closed the sale, collectively they're dynamite. When you have mastered these questions and use them, closing will be the easiest part of the sale. Won't it?

A brief word of caution. Don't overdo it. Don't make it too obvious. It's another technique that practice makes perfect, so you should make a game of it until it becomes natural and easy, shouldn't you? You will, won't you?

A second caution. Questioning does no good if you don't listen to the answer — even to a minor question. Ask. Listen. Every time.

When you can get the customer to say yes to each sales point as you go along, the close comes naturally. Another series of questions (even more powerful when they are used with skill) works best when you agree with a customer's statement and then ask her to agree with you. Here's how it works:

CUSTOMER: Oh my, that is soft!

SALESPERSON: Yes, it is, isn't it?

Any time your customer makes a positive statement you must support it and get her to reaffirm it. Again, it requires a little concentrated practice but it will soon become second nature to you.

▶
> SALESPERSON: Boy, that sales book by John F. Lawhon is the best book ever written on selling!
>
> YOU: It certainly is, isn't it?

These techniques should be a part of your everyday vocabulary. And not just when you are selling, right? When used constantly in normal conversation, they will come as a natural part of your presentation, won't they? The natural extension of these questions is to shift them around to permit you more flexibility. Some examples are:

> Won't they be perfect?
>
> Isn't this exactly what we discussed?
>
> Aren't they the perfect length?
>
> And so on.

Another questioning technique that should be second nature to you is answering a customer's questions with questions of your own.

Here is how many salespeople would answer a customer's questions.

> CUSTOMER: Do you have it in blue?
>
> SALESPERSON: No.

> CUSTOMER: Do you deliver on Saturday?
>
> SALESPERSON: No.

> CUSTOMER: Does it have an ice-maker?
>
> SALESPERSON: Yes.

> CUSTOMER: Does it come with extra leaves?
>
> SALESPERSON: YES.

Try the same questions this way. (It takes practice, but the payoff is worth it.)

CUSTOMER: Do you have it in blue?

SALESPERSON: Is this the one you want if you can get it in blue?

CUSTOMER: Do you deliver on Saturday?

SALESPERSON: Is there an important reason for having it delivered on Saturday?

CUSTOMER: Does this have an ice-maker?

SALESPERSON: Is an ice-maker important to you?

CUSTOMER: Does it come with extra leaves?

SALESPERSON: Would this be the right table for you if it had extra leaves?

These four examples point out that whether your answer is yes or no, you convert that answer to a closing question. You can always keep the sale going by asking a question instead of saying no.

These few techniques alone can add thousands of dollars to your earnings every year. Salespeople who use them weren't born with them. They learned them and practiced them. So can you.

If there is one area of sales questions that salespeople agree on, it is the importance of asking "your choice" questions. When you can naturally ask questions that require an answer from your customer other than yes or no, then and only then are you on the road to selling success.

> No! Stops the sale dead if you aren't quick on your feet. It's all over when the customer says no! Given a choice of saying yes or no to a salesperson, the great majority of customers are going to say no! Professionals avoid this word with a simple technique. They ask questions that lead the customer to say yes, while not giving them the option of saying no.

A customer may be polite and say, "Let me think about it, I'll let you know tomorrow," or "I have to ask my great uncle," or any one of a thousand other excuses which all boil down to no.

Professionals reduce the chances of hearing a no by practicing good techniques. We have seen how the professional reduces the nos in the approach; even more in the qualifying and selection phases. The professional practically eliminates any chance of a no with his "can't you?," "won't you?," "don't you agree?" questions during the presentation. Throughout, he remains on guard as he asks questions by avoiding those that call for yes or no answers.

> "Your choice" questions work like this:
>
> "If you decide on this one, will you want it in red or blue?"
>
> "If you buy this one, will you want to use one of our credit plans or will you pay cash?"
>
> "Our regular delivery date is next Monday. If you purchase today, would that be soon enough? Or will you need it before that date?

As you can see, these examples get you closer to the sale while exposing any objections the customer might have. They literally eliminate any possibility of encountering that terrible word NO!

Most sales books have lots of material on questioning techniques. The more you read, the more you study, the more you practice, the more sales you are going to make and the more easily you are going to make them. ANY QUESTIONS?

> NOTE: It might have occurred to you in reading this chapter that the need for most of these questions would have been eliminated if the salesperson had done a better job of qualifying. You're right!

31

Phase Four: Presenting

OVERCOMING OBJECTIONS

Properly handled, most customer objections are actually steps to the sale. However, some objections are statements of conditions that preclude a sale. That seldom happens in retailing, but you have to understand what's behind those objections so you don't waste time trying to sell when no sale *can* be made.

Here are a few conditions that would preclude you from making a sale, because *impossible dream equals impossible sale.*

A young lady comes into your store to buy a door mirror for her apartment, which she shares with a roommate. Both work at a fast food restaurant as counter girls. She sees a $4,000 French bedroom group featuring a king-sized bed with an eight-foot-high canopy.

Four conditions preclude her purchase of that bedroom group:

1. No money.
2. No way to get the money.
3. No place to put the furniture.
4. No way to get a place for it.

Of course, you oh and ah over the group along with your customer, but it would be foolish to spend hours of your time trying to sell it. Even though there is hardly anything your customer wouldn't do to get the bedroom suite.

Here is where the order taker really shines because he can't tell the difference between a customer with existing conditions that preclude her buying and one with only a minor objection.

Now! / 37

And here comes an amazing phenomenon: usually, the most expensive item is what customers dream of owning, while realizing they probably never will. When they see these items in real life they go ga-ga over them. Of course, they want them. Of course, they would like to own them. Of course, they would like to buy them, but they can't!

This never occurs to the order taker. He understands nothing about a sale. All he understands is the commission on a large order. So the order taker will waste hours, days, and weeks on the impossible dream which is an equally impossible sale.

Order takers will go to any length to get the customer to carry on with this farce, often even writing up the sale with a C.O.D. down payment. When the credit department turns down the sale, the order taker spends hours and days trying to get the customer to bring in a co-signer or promise a larger C.O.D. down payment, sometimes even putting it on layaway and keeping the dream alive a little longer. If he has weak management (many order takers do) the manager gets caught up in the dream and, he too, goes along with the fantasy.

These ridiculous situations can continue indefinitely if not brought to a halt by the accounting office. You can believe it or not, but right now in retail stores across America there are hundreds of millions of dollars' worth of sales just like this one. Just as ridiculous, just as impossible.

They'll stay on the books as long as any pretense can be found for keeping them there. Mostly, they are big sales, but there also are plenty of little ones. Some have been on the books a day or two, some a week or two, many a month or two. You wouldn't have to look too far to find some that have been on the books a year or two. Anytime you ask an order taker why a sale is on the books, he will always assure you it is a good sale and has only a minor problem to overcome.

Here's the sad part: I really believe that the order taker and the customer both get so carried away by their dream that they are sincere in hoping against hope a miracle will take place and the sale will really happen.

It won't!

If you are a beginner and you think this story is an exception among order takers or that it is an exaggeration, it's not. If you want to hear about more sales like this, just follow an order taker masquerading as a salesperson into the lounge. The dream sale is the kind he loves to brag about.

THE ORDER TAKER TURNS TRAITOR

When the order taker first writes up this kind of "sale," he boasts to one and all about how he turned a $10 mirror customer into an $4,000 order. Then when the credit department turns it down, he complains about what a stupid credit manager the company has. "What good does it do to make a sale when the credit department turns it down anyway?" When the order taker rewrites the sale and puts it into layaway with the entire balance C.O.D., he crows about how he saved the sale after everybody in the company had tried to kill it. Truth eventually wins out and the fantasy order is canceled, with the order taker moaning, groaning, blaming everyone in the company and even the customer. Incredible as it seems, this is a common occurrence.

Some order takers even get flip about it. You will hear them say, "I just throw everything I can write up against the wall and see what sticks."

This kind of make-believe is coming to a stop because the cost of doing business is going up so fast that wasted time is too expensive a luxury for retailers to afford and because the computer is making such selling obvious. Humoring the order taker is definitely on the way out.

SOME OBJECTIONS ARE LEGITIMATE

An objection to buying may be a legitimate reason why the customer cannot and will not buy. For example, the customer may say, "That color wouldn't go with a thing in my living room." Or, "There is no way we could afford the payments since I had to quit working to have the baby." Or, "My husband is a mechanic. If I came home with that white silk sofa, he would throw us both out."

These objections surface in the qualifying phase of the sale. The professional rarely if ever gets sidetracked on this type of situation. He recognizes a true condition and accepts it, wasting no time chasing rainbows.

The professional knows his job is to cause real dreams to come true.

UNCONDITIONAL SURRENDER
FOR THE ORDER TAKER

Because the order taker never develops the skills needed to become a salesperson, he can't recognize a sale-killing condition. Amazingly, he understands even less the objection, which is merely a request for the buying information that will lead to a sale.

I say "amazingly," because the order taker, as you have just seen, will chase an impossible objection for days, weeks, months, even years, but he will drop a sale at the first little objection the customer has, even though the objection was really just a request for product information.

We have already seen the order taker in action with his "Can I help you?" and the customer's objection to being helped with a "No thanks, I am just looking."

Bang. The order taker accepts that and heads for the lounge. Now let's look at him in action when he finally gets to make a presentation.

> CUSTOMER: I think this one is too large.
>
> ORDER TAKER: Let's look for something smaller.
>
> CUSTOMER: This one is too dark.
>
> ORDER TAKER: Let's look for a lighter one.
>
> CUSTOMER: I want to think it over.
>
> ORDER TAKER: Fine, here's my card.
>
> CUSTOMER: I didn't want to spend that much.
>
> ORDER TAKER: Let me show you some lower-priced items.

As you can see, the failure possibilities are endless for the hapless order taker.

If he works so hard on the $4,000 impossible sale why does he quit on the first minor objection during a solid sale?

The only reason for not making any sale is a condition that makes it literally impossible for the customer to buy or use your product.

The order taker never admits that making the sale was his job so when the sale is lost, he will not assume responsibility for losing it.

He can spend hours blaming conditions and other people for every lost sale.

We have seen how the order taker reacts to a minor objection and how he will not take any blame for losing the sale. Now, let's watch a professional handling the minor objections that lead to a sale.

THE CUSTOMER WANTS TO OWN

Professionals understand what an objection really is. They realize their job is to supply the information that the customer needs to make the best buying decision. *When a customer makes a minor objection, the pro hears "I am interested in buying your product, but I need more information before I will buy."* ◀

> CUSTOMER: I think the finish is too dark.
>
> Salesperson: Why?
>
> CUSTOMER: It won't match my woodwork.
>
> SALESPERSON: Is it important that it match your woodwork?
>
> CUSTOMER: Well, come to think of it, I guess not.

The customer was trying to put off making the decision and wanted more assurance that his choice would get the approval he needed. The salesperson's job is to lead the customer to that decision, not to abandon him by saying: "Let me show you something lighter."

> CUSTOMER: I want to think it over.
>
> SALESPERSON: Of course, you must be sure you are doing the right thing when your decision is so important to your family, mustn't you?
>
> CUSTOMER: Yes, I want to be really sure before I buy.
>
> SALESPERSON: Mrs. Smith, before you leave, let's review how this product will meet your needs, just so you have it fresh in your mind.

In this case, the customer has simply said, "I don't think I have enough information to make this decision." She has said "I need your product, I want your product, please give me more information so I can be more confident. Then I will buy your product."

When you feel you have told the customer everything you have to tell and demonstrated everything there is to demonstrate, your tendency will be to agree with the customer's objection and give him your card.

Don't do it!

As long as you have a "maybe" from your customer, keep selling. Don't quit.

It's at this point that the professional buckles down and gets the sale by saying, "Mrs. Jones, so that all of the features will be fresh in your mind, let's review them." And then, quite simply, he starts over.

▶ Remember, no customer digests every part of your presentation. But when you repeat it, reinforcing what she has learned and digested, you get another chance to establish solidly those benefits she missed the first time.

> **The professional knows he will normally have to repeat part or all of his presentation more than once before all objections are overcome and the sale is made. Just because he has said it once does not guarantee that the customer either heard or understood it, and often he must repeat something many times before it is fully established in the customer's mind.**

CUSTOMER: I am sorry but I just think it is too expensive.

SALESPERSON: Let me repeat your objection to be sure I understand it. You say you feel the sofa is expensive. May I ask why? (Note: Salesperson omitted the "too.")

CUSTOMER: I just didn't want to spend that much money.

SALESPERSON: Of course, you could buy a lower-priced sofa, but you would have to give up a lot of the important features that you really need. Don't you agree?

With that, the professional salesperson proceeds to review his or her presentation, re-emphasizing the benefits of each feature.

> CUSTOMER: You say I will have to wait thirty days to get this sofa in blue. I think I would rather go back to the other store and buy the one I saw there.
>
> SALESPERSON: Did you like the one you saw there better than this one?
>
> CUSTOMER: No, but they have it in stock and I can have it now.
>
> SALESPERSON: Mrs. Jones, how long do you expect your new sofa to last?
>
> CUSTOMER: At least ten years.
>
> SALESPERSON: Mrs. Jones, is having a sofa you don't like two or three weeks earlier more important than having the sofa you really like, the one that does more of everything you want it to do, the one you really want? When you consider living with and using it for ten years, those few extra days you have to wait will make you love this sofa even more once it's in your home. Let's go back to the office and see if we can't get a better delivery date for you.

All these objections are disguised requests for additional information that will lead the customer to the right buying decision.

It's obvious how the order taker and the salesperson respond to the same situation, isn't it?

The order taker never has the information needed to overcome objections. So he has no choice but to switch products and hope no objection will arise on the second selection. But objections will arise; they do almost every time.

No Luck in Selling

The order taker consoles himself by whining that he would outsell the top salesperson if he could get even a few of the really good customers, but all he gets is lookers. "Most customers don't know what they need, leave without buying, and are so stupid they don't even know what they want!" he raves to anyone foolish enough to listen. Luck has nothing to do with it.

Now, do you see why you can't afford the negative contamination of that order taker who masquerades as a salesperson?

When you have the five groups of knowledge at your command, the good objection is a sure sign that the sale is yours.

> **HERE IS A VITALLY IMPORTANT NOTE!**
> I can't say this often enough: The great majority of the objections a customer makes to buying can be avoided by a good job of qualifying.

Phase Four: Presenting

OBJECTION INSIGHT

As you practice your skills and begin to realize what selling really is, an entirely new sense of confidence takes over. You'll be like a kid again, and there's no thrill like it because it will affect every act you undertake.

Order takers twist down the road to lost sales because they have no plan, map, direction, skill, or knowledge to do otherwise. They are involved in the hardest low-paying work there is.

The professional salesperson knows every step of the way to a sale. At no time does he ever doubt he is on the right road because he knows he has the knowledge and skills needed to lead the customer all the way down that road to its end — the sale.

Don't forget two very important things about objections. Grasp of the five basic groups of knowledge gives you the ability to handle any objection once it surfaces, but your skills in qualifying and selecting can eliminate many minor objections before they arise. It's great to be able to overcome minor objections, but the professional either keeps only the ones he wants to use or eliminates every one during qualifying.

PLANTING OBJECTIONS

Years ago, I was discussing income tax with a wealthy man. He was very honest about filing his returns, but he said, "John, when the IRS agent audits your return, he is not going to be satisfied if he can't find two or three things to disallow. I always put three small deductions in my return which I know he will find and throw out. Invariably, when he has found them he is happy and the audit is over. Otherwise, he goes on looking forever, trying to find something."

A sale can be like that — sometimes you need ways to get the customer to say yes if you are to do your job. Once he needs and wants your product, it is your job to help him get it. If that means helping him say yes, then that's your job. The great ones get good at this by sometimes planting objections for the customer to find which will make getting the yes that much easier.

For example, early in the sale the salesperson will plant an objection.

"Mrs. Jones, should we find something that meets your needs, I want you to know that we deliver free on a seven-day schedule."

When he has made his presentation and wants a trial close, he says:

"Mrs. Jones, as I mentioned earlier, should you buy this sofa we deliver it free and can have it in your home by one week from today. Would that be soon enough or would you need it sooner?"

If she says, "One week would be okay but, of course, if I bought it I would like to have it sooner." Then the professional moves right in (as he had planned from the beginning) with: "Why don't I check to see if I could have it delivered tomorrow? Maybe there has been a last-minute change in someone else's delivery."

He heads for the office, knowing that if she doesn't stop him the sale is made.

The professional not only handles objections by realizing they are requests for information, but he also learns to plant objections to help the customer make or confirm his buying decision.

Learning to use delivery dates can be a valuable tool if done honestly. Most companies have a two- or three-day local delivery schedule. That means only that they cannot process the order and deliver the purchase sooner than that. It does not mean that their purchase cannot be delivered in five days, ten days, or even 30 days. One thing the professional knows about the customer is that once he buys an item he would like to have it delivered at once and have it waiting for him at his home when he arrives.

Of course, that is seldom possible, so the professional, knowing the customer will object even to a next-day delivery, anticipates the objection and uses it to his advantage.

Weak salespeople I interviewed cited their company's delivery program as a major reason for their losing sales. Order takers lose millions of dollars in sales because they can't deliver soon enough, while the same factor is the strongest sales-getter in the professional's bag. He knows the power of using the objection as an order-clincher when it's part of his plan.

The professional knows what objections to anticipate and makes plans not just to overcome them, but to trade the solution to the objection for an agreement to buy.

When we used to sell three-room groups of furniture with used appliances, the strongest and surest way to get the sale was to price the group with used appliances high enough so that when you got to the close, you said, "You both seem to agree that you like all the furniture, the price is fine, you can easily handle the payments, but the only thing you don't like is the used appliances."

Of course, they always said yes.

The salesperson then said, "If I could get the manager to let you have the new range and refrigerator from the group that costs $300 more instead of the used range and refrigerator in this group, is there any reason why you would not buy today?" It was a rare customer who didn't jump at the opportunity.

INTEGRITY QUESTIONED

Most people today might question the ethics of this strategy, so let's examine it further.

> **The objective is to make a sale that is only completed when you have a happy and satisfied customer enjoying the benefits of your product. I question any selling strategy that does not result in a satisfied customer or does not have as its top priority a satisfied customer.**

Market strategy, which is at the base of every great product or company, is the ultimate reason for their successes. You may have a better product and a better price, but if your competitors are using strategies that are taking the sales away from you, your days and your product's days are numbered.

When some supermarkets raised prices a tiny fraction on some items not easily spotted by the average customer so they could give out savings stamps, it started taking business from other companies.

They, in turn, started giving savings stamps to get their customers back and to hold onto those they still had.

When they all had savings stamps that added two or three percent to the price of their goods, then one chain proclaimed it had done away with the high cost of stamps and was offering its goods at greatly reduced prices. And so the battle for the consumer dollar continued.

Today, marketing and advertising has been greatly refined, but whether we like it or not, "free" is still the most powerful word in advertising and "sale" is the second most powerful. Each professional develops his own set of selling strategies according to his personal ethics, but I can assure you that if those ethics require that you lie, or if their deployment does not result in a satisfied customer, they are wrong and they will fail.

Select the company you are going to sell for based on its policies and strategies. Many companies today will dicker on price and many great professionals love this kind of selling climate. I sold a lot of furniture and appliances for companies that negotiated price when I was younger. My own experience has led me to believe that no company is really well grounded if its price lacks integrity, and the professional salesperson working for a company that has a fixed price selling head-to-head against the variable-price store will get the sale every time if all else is equal.

The professional who does not intend to use price cutting as a crutch when he comes to the close will do a better job of selling his product.

▶ *When the professional creates many benefits and the final decision is made in a competitive situation, it is not the price that will decide the sale, but the benefits promised for the price.*

No Commission for Competitor's Sale

One very unusual quirk of human nature shows up when people bring up an objection during a sale. The odds are that the first objection is not the real objection. For example, a customer says, "We really like this sofa, but we want to think about it and look around."

Now that's an objection to buying right now. The real reason they want to think about it is because once you have helped them find the sofa they want in the cover and color they can use and want, they want to look elsewhere to see if they can get it at a better price.

When you give up on that objection — which is not the real objection — the odds are you sold the sofa for someone else. It is a rare company that, when facing the possibility of losing a sale because a competitor has a better price, will not meet or beat that price.

Many times, after your competitor beats your price, killing your sale in the process, he then proceeds to convince your customers that the sofa you selected was not the best for them. Most of the time he then switches your customers to an even higher-priced sofa and gets the sale, having already established that he has the best prices in comparison with your sofa and price.

The professional knows he must make the sale while the customer ◀ is still in the store or take very long odds on it. The professional also knows most first objections are smokescreens thrown up to hide a real objection. He will always hear out every objection.

Mark this: Any time your customer starts an objection, *hear him* ◀ *out*, Never interrupt. Let him complete his objection and do not argue.

THE TERRIBLE "TOOS"

When you ask why, the customer will almost always respond with a "too."

It's too big.

It's too small.

It costs too much.

The first thing you must do is get rid of the "too" and then the objection is easy to overcome. As long as the "too" remains, you won't make the sale.

So let's attack "too" and learn how to get rid of it. You are going to be surprised at how easy it is.

The customer says no.

You ask why?

The customer says it's "too" big.

You repeat the customer's objection back to him: "You say it is big?" All you have done is gotten rid of the "too." Now you have reduced the objection to just being big. "Big" is not bad; "too big" is bad, so all we have to do now is show that big is good to overcome the objection and ask for the order again.

When you have done a reasonable job of qualifying the customer's problem, it is rare that you will ever hear more than one "too." Now, the most common "toos" of all:

> SALESPERSON: Why?
> CUSTOMER: It's too expensive.
> SALESPERSON: You say it is expensive?

Wow!!! When the "too" is gone we have a very simple job on our hands. There is a world of difference between an expensive sofa and a sofa that is "too" expensive. Just review the need and show how the customer would not consider a product that fails to meet the need as well or as completely even though it was *less* expensive, and the sale is made.

Maybe you never thought about the word "too." When the customer says something is "too," the dictionary says the customer means "in a degree beyond expression or endurance." As long as the customer's objection is expressed as "too" anything, there can be no solution. And when the "too" is in fact a genuine "too," no sale will result. For example:

> CUSTOMER: That dresser is too long.
>
> SALESPERSON: You say the dresser is long?
>
> CUSTOMER: No, I said it is too long. The only wall I have in my bedroom for a dresser is 63 inches. That dresser is 74 inches and it is too long.

Now that is what you call a genuine "too," but you should have determined the size of that wall during qualifying. See why failure to qualify can haunt you later in your sale, often when it is *too* late?

You are going to hear this excuse for not buying now thousands of times in your sales career. "I will have to go home and measure to be sure I have enough room."

If you are getting genuine "toos" to your "why?" questions, it is because you didn't execute the previous phases of your sale properly. When you get a genuine "too" while you are trying to close the sale, the odds are you will lose it.

A genuine "too" is a dead end. Never, never, never try to overcome a genuine "too." You will only alienate the customer.

The professional has one great quality the order taker doesn't. When the professional realizes he has made a mistake, he quickly admits it, apologizes, and offers to correct it. That's why he can get the sale even when he gets a genuine "too" during the closing.

Here's how the professionals do it.

> CUSTOMER: It's too big. The only wall I have in my bedroom for a dresser is 63 inches long. That dresser is 74 inches long.
>
> SALESPERSON: Mrs. Jones, I am so sorry. That's my fault for not asking you the length of your wall before I wasted your time and got you all excited about a bedroom group you could not use. Would you forgive me and let me show you only those bedroom groups which would fit the dimensions of your room?

This is the only approach that can turn a genuine "too" into a sale.

Assuming you have only received a "too" to your "why?" question and it's not a genuine "too," simply restate the customer's objection without the "too."

> CUSTOMER: The sofa is too expensive.
>
> SALESPERSON: Mrs. Jones, let me repeat your objection just to be sure I clearly understand. You say the sofa is expensive?

Once the "too" is gone, if it wasn't a genuine "too," it won't come back. You can now proceed.

After you have answered the objection to the customer's complete satisfaction, be sure you have the customer's agreement with a question like:

> **That seems to answer that question, doesn't it?"**
> **I guess we have covered that, haven't we?"**
> **That was the answer you needed for that question, wasn't it?"**

You do feel that we have completely covered that, don't you?"

Only when the customer agrees with a nod or a "yes," do you go forward with the sale. Not before.

THINK ABOUT THIS:
Not one of the objections discussed in this chapter will come up if the salesperson does a good job of qualifying the customers' needs and desires.

Phase Four: Presenting

OVERCOMING MONEY OBJECTIONS

Is It The Money?

When an objection is a smokescreen, you must get through to the real objection with more probing questions.

Remember, a customer who wants to leave without buying has not been sold because there are still unresolved objections to his buying now. Unless you can root them out and answer them, you are not going to make a sale. Almost without exception, if there is a final objection, it will be the cost, the one objection every retail customer is most embarrassed to bring up.

It can usually be ferreted out with this question: "In addition to that (whatever the objection was), isn't there some other reason for your not buying now?"

Obviously, when you have answered or encouraged the customers to answer every objection they had to buying now and they still haven't bought, there must be an unvoiced objection, don't you agree? Well, you can't afford to let even one go unspoken or you lose the sale.

Don't quit now! You have tried diplomacy and failed; before you lose the sale, you had better ask the big question: "Is it the money?"

Look the customer right in the eye and it's like catching a kid with his hand in the cookie jar. Nearly every time, the customer is going to answer meekly, "Well, to be honest with you, that's it."

Whoopee!!! That's it! The final objection — overcome it and the sale is yours! (See closing techniques for handling the money question.)

The longer you are in sales, the more you will become convinced that a few moments just before your customer says yes a mild form of insanity takes over. The customer goes through a period of decision making and as the time for the final answer approaches, he may say some very strange things. Usually, this final resistance to saying yes is voiced as an unreasonable objection.

As you come to understand better what is actually happening, you'll learn not to show any reaction while the customer vents his feelings. When he gets it out of his system, it's almost like a catharsis. If you have the patience, you'll find he's a little embarrassed when he says, "I guess we will take it."

Most often, you'll encounter this when you have the husband and wife together. She is encouraging him to buy the furniture the family needs and he is trying to get out of it so the money can be spent on something of his choice for his pleasure. Sometimes, as you are waiting for the answer to your closing question under circumstances like these, when the silence is deafening, all of a sudden the husband will jump up and literally start railing at his wife. "I told you when we came down here that we were just going to look." As he paces back and forth, his voice will rise. "I have no intention of spending that much money. You know better than to have gotten me into this. What's the matter with you, anyway?"

Just about the time you think he is going to slug you, her, or one of the kids, he melts and slides back into one of the chairs, sits silently for a moment, and says meekly, "If she really wants it, let her have it."

I have seen this pattern occur thousands of times. Believe me, it's a very normal psychological phenomenon. Just ride it out in silence, showing no alarm, and the sale is yours every time. The husband generally trails along submissively while the order is being written and never says another word. It may sound strange, but no more so than all the other crazy, exciting things that will happen in your life as a salesperson.

JUST SUPPOSE

CUSTOMER: This mattress is too hard.

SALESPERSON: Mrs. Jones, I am sure you're right when you say that this mattress is hard. (Note: the "too" is gone.) Would you just suppose that after sleeping on it for 30 nights the morning backaches you have been having would be gone and you'd be getting a better night's sleep than you have in years? If that happened, would you still believe it was too hard?

The magic question begins "Just suppose . . ."

If you can get the customer to put aside his unreasonable objection for a moment, you can go on with your sale. By the time you complete your presentation, the objection will not come up again.

"You see, Mrs. Jones, it's likely that your backaches are from lack of support and we know that it will take an orthopedic-type mattress, which is much firmer than the one you are sleeping on now, to eliminate the pains. We also know that it will take you a few nights to get used to the firmer bed. That's why we make this free offer. We are sure that after sleeping on this bed for 30 nights your backaches, if they were due to lack of support, will be gone and you will be sleeping better. But after the 30-day trial if you are not completely satisfied, we will give you a full refund. After all, you can't lose anything but your backache on a deal like that, can you? Let's get it out to your home right away and get you sleeping better, okay?"

See how you can "Just suppose . . ." your way to a sale?

These words can make you thousands of dollars in commissions. Suppose you used them? Suppose you made more sales? Suppose you made more commissions because you "supposed" your way into more sales? Now, I suppose that would be exciting, don't you?

Just suppose . . . Use these exact words.

YES, BUT —

Another traditional technique for handling objections is the "yes, but" approach. It works like this:

"Yes, I agree that the nap is deeper on the other carpet, but this one has a much tighter weave. It will far outwear the other carpet, but equally important is that with your three growing boys dirt and food particles will get down into that deeper shag pile and it is almost impossible to shampoo or vacuum them out. With this shorter nap and tighter weave, cleaning and shampooing is much easier. That would be an important consideration, wouldn't it?"

In other words, you agree that the customer is right. The nap on the other carpet is longer, but the feature of your carpet offers benefits far more important to her than the longer nap. As a matter of fact, you have changed what seemed important to her only moments before into something that she wouldn't have in her home now.

"Yes, but" is a tried and true technique that will make you sales when all else fails. And think of all the exciting commissions it can mean to you!

False Objections

What do you do when the customer makes an objection that is not true? You can't say, "I agree with you," can you? Of course not. You might think that when a customer makes an out-and-out false objection, it would be even easier to overcome. Wrong! As a matter of fact, it's a lot harder, and improperly handled, can lose the sale every time.

The first time I learned that winning an argument often meant losing the sale was one of the most traumatic lessons of my selling experiences. When I was in my early 20s I owned two small furniture stores. A local bank carried all my credit accounts. Because a large portion of my business was sold on credit and financed at the only bank in town, if the bank refused to finance my customers I was out of business.

The banker had a son who cost me a very large sale by telling a customer something that was simply not true. I was livid. I raced to the bank and in my righteous indignation told the banker's son just how wrong he was, proving my point to everyone's satisfaction. I won that argument hands down.

One-half hour after I returned to my office, an officer of the only bank in town arrived and informed me that the bank would no longer carry my customer's accounts.

Oh, I was dead right and dead broke at the same time. I can assure you that I had to be taught that lesson only once.

Put this down on a 3 x 5 card right now:

You can win an argument with a customer, but you'll lose the sale. And that is *not* the name of the game. The purpose of your profession is to make sales.

Then how do you avoid an argument when the customer challenges you, your company, or your product with a false and damaging statement? Here is an example:

> CUSTOMER: You salespeople are all alike. You'll say anything to get a sale.
>
> ORDER TAKER: Mister, are you calling me a liar? (That sale is over.)
>
> PROFESSIONAL SALESPERSON: Wow! That's a tough one, Mr. Jones. Let me repeat it to be sure I understand it. You say that all salespeople will say anything to get a sale?
>
> CUSTOMER: That's right!
>
> PROFESSIONAL SALESPERSON: I'm sure you have a good reason for feeling that way. Do you mind if I ask what it is?

Do you know that 99% of the time, the customer will start backtracking by saying: "Well, I am sure you're not that way, but I have had some salespeople wait on me . . . etc., etc." After a few more words, the customer will be happy to change the subject and forget all about his statement because as soon as he starts explaining why he feels that way, he realizes how foolish his statement really was. Your gracious willingness to forget it and get on with the sale will be greatly appreciated.

I picked the hardest single objection a salesperson will ever face for that example. If you can handle that one, you can handle any of them.

Here are six powerful words that are an important part of any professional salesperson's life: Who? What? Where? When? Why? How?

When you are at an absolute loss for words, any one of these will come to your rescue. If dog is man's best friend, these six words — who, what, when, where, why, and how — are the salesperson's best friend.

(The order taker rarely uses them because he doesn't have the five groups of knowledge he needs to handle the customer's request for answers these words initiate.)

One of the wonderful traits of human nature is that we all like to be authorities. When we have the information to handle objections, we are anxious to hear them, knowing the sale is ours. When our customers recognize us as authorities, our success becomes even sweeter.

I Can Get It for Less

Next to "I am just looking," you will hear variations of this statement most often: "I can get it for less."

If you have been in sales very long you know that sometimes the customer who says this is telling the truth, sometimes he is lying, sometimes he is wrong but thinks he's right.

Let's examine that statement in depth and see how the professional salesperson handles it.

"Your price is too high." This one is really different from "I can get it for less" but let's check the two together.

When he's being truthful, the customer who has said "Your price is too high" really means "Based on what you have told me, the features and benefits of your product are not worth to me the amount of money you are asking."

In other words, the customer is saying that you are offering a little

bitty pile of benefits and asking for a great big old pile of money. He means, "Now, if you can't show me and tell me about more benefits your product can give me and my family, you are not going to get me to buy your product."

When this customer said your price was too high, he was really asking for more information. If you can't supply it, you are not going to get the sale.

Let's say you have shown a sofa to a family and everyone likes it. They all think it's great. You ask for the order, and the husband says, "Your price it too high." First, you review the benefits you promised and then in a lowered, quizzical voice, you ask him, "Mr. Jones, you say my price is high. Do you mind if I ask why?" (Note the missing "too.")

> MR. JONES: Well, we can get a sofa almost exactly like this one down the street for $100 less.
>
> SALESPERSON: Mr. Jones, I am well acquainted with that sofa and for the price they are asking it's a good value. But its quality is not to be compared with our sofa. May I tell you why? Is it the price of the sofa that bothers you or the cost of the sofa?
>
> MR. JONES: What do you mean, price or cost? Your sofa price is $599. If I buy it, it will cost me $599 and price or cost, that's too high and more than I want to spend.
>
> SALESPERSON: Mr. Jones, suppose for one minute that you buy the sofa from our competitors for $499. Would you expect it to last as long as ours would with your three boys and all their friends using it?
>
> CUSTOMER: I suppose not.
>
> SALESPERSON: Let's suppose you buy a new suit of clothes for $200 on sale. From a hundred feet away, no one could tell it from a $500 suit. But within two or three cleanings, your $200 suit starts losing its shape and after three or four months the seams in the seat give out, the waist band starts to roll up, the suit gets uncomfortable to wear, and before the first year is out, you quit wearing it because it looks exactly like what it is — a cheap suit.

Now, the $500 suit is so well constructed and of such a superior fabric that it feels comfortable when you buy it and the longer you wear it the more comfortable it gets. But even more importantly, it had a quality look when you got it. It kept that look for five, six or seven years in spite of how often you wore it. And as the fabric finally starts to give way, you hate to give it up because it has become so comfortable over the years.

Now Mr. Jones, the *price* of the $200 suit broke down into a *cost* of $200 a year and it did not give pride, comfort, or a quality look during that year of use.

Mr. Jones, the $500 suit that felt so good, looked so good, make you feel so good, stayed as good and looked as good as new for five years, that suit cost you $100 a year. One more thing, Mr. Jones, you probably wore the $500 suit twice as often as the lesser-priced, uncomfortable suit. It breaks down this way: the cost per year of the $500 suit was one-half the cost per year of the $200 suit, but the cost per time you wore it was a quarter the cost of the $200 suit.

More important than that, Mr. Jones, you can't put a price on the comfort and pride you felt when you wore the $500 suit.

So let me ask you, Mr. Jones, was it price or cost that concerned you?

COST VS. PRICE

You can't become a really top professional salesperson until you understand cost and price. They are not the same.

In 1971, my wife and I stopped at a Rolls Royce showroom in Costa Mesa, California. There were two new Corniche convertibles. The window stickers were about $32,000; the salesman offered me my choice for $28,000. I was then driving a 1971 Jaguar XKE for which I had paid $7,200. The owner of the Rolls Royce dealership told me if I would buy the new Corniche convertible, he would give me a contract guarantee that at the end of five years he would pay me the $28,000 for the car. I thought he was crazy, and did not buy the car even though I could afford it because the price was too high.

In 1972, a year after I bought the XKE, I sold it for $4,000. It had cost me $3,200 for the one year I had had it.

By 1976, that 1971 Rolls Convertible was selling for around $40,000. It would have cost me nothing to have owned it for five years. As a matter of fact, I would have realized a profit of almost $3,000 a year.

This is one of the best examples I can give you to illustrate the difference between price and cost.

Because the customer knows only the price of an item (and price translated into cost is often an entirely different number), *you* must understand the difference and be able to help your customer understand it, if you are truly going to master selling.

The number one objection to your product will always be the *price* until you have mastered the six phases of the sale.

Here are a few more examples.

When I first met my wife, she was a successful executive in a large advertising agency, even though she was only 24 years old. She was then and is now one of the best-dressed women I know. I found it hard to understand why she bought only the very finest of design and quality when she shopped for new things. They seemed so expensive. It took me many years to realize that the cost of my wife's clothes is one of the most reasonable items in our budget.

The quality and style of her clothes is so well selected that at almost any time anything in her wardrobe looks like the very latest style. And the quality keeps her clothes looking as if she were wearing them for the first time even after five, six, seven — and more years than she'll permit me to tell.

A comparison:

> The cost of the $200 dress was $200 a year.
> The cost of the $800 dress was $160 a year, but can you imagine what that $800 dress does for a woman's sense of pride and self-worth?

Of course, right now I can hear someone who is reading this book say, "Yeah, but who wants a dress to last five years?"

DRESS

Price: $800	Price $200
(Worn five years and still new and very much in style; because of its comfort it gets worn twice as often.)	(Worn one year; out of style and looks worn out.)

Of course, the woman who bought the $200 dress doesn't want *that* dress to last five years, but the woman who was helped by a professional salesperson to buy the right $800 dress loves it so much that she never wants to see it wear out because each year it becomes more comfortable. Every time she wears it, it makes her feel prettier and people always notice that and compliment her on how nice she looks. She is even motivated to take care of her figure so she can continue to wear this wonderful garment.

Wait a minute, I'm not implying my wife has only one dress, or that it cost $800, but she has built her wardrobe very well over the years and she has never said to me, "I don't have a thing to wear." I dare say the cost per year of her clothes is much less than that of most women at her income level.

Let's say you bought the lowest-priced tire you could find for your family car. You chose between one that was $50 and another for $100. To keep it simple, let's say the $100 tire will wear twice as long as the $50 one.

The real benefit you get from the $100 tire is safety because of the greatly reduced chance of tire failure. If peace of mind alone was considered the benefit and during the life of both tires you never had a tire failure, the $100 tire was still a far better value.

Let's "for instance" for a moment.

Say a tire failure resulted in the tragic death of one of your children.

If you had bought the cheaper tire you would carry to your grave guilt about your buying decision. If the finest tire that you could buy had failed you, then there'd be no guilt.

When we say the responsibility of the professional salesperson is to furnish all the information the customer needs to make the best buying decision, this is what we mean. Would you feel no sense of responsibility for that child's death if as a tire salesperson you had failed to convince the parents of the best tire buy which was also the lowest *cost* tire, even though it didn't have the lowest *price*?

Benjamin Franklin tells about a time when he was four or five years old and was among several older boys, one of whom had a new tin whistle that was the center of attention. He had to have that tin whistle. He felt that if he had it he'd become the center of attention and all of those older boys would want to be his friend.

So he raced home, shook the few pennies from his piggy bank, gathered up a couple of his treasures, and rushed back to where the older boys were playing. Without further ado, he told the boy with the whistle he would give him seven pennies and two toys for the whistle. His offer was grabbed up immediately.

When the sale was completed, the other kids ridiculed him with "Why did you give him seven pennies and two toys for that tin whistle when you can buy those whistles for one penny at the toy shop?" Ben Franklin vowed never again to pay too much for a whistle. Maybe you have never heard this story, but I bet you have heard his famous saying, A penny saved is a penny earned. Now you know where he learned it.

Here was a classic case of the price being too high, yet if the whistle had made Ben the center of attention, if it had made the big boys his friends, he could have paid even more for it and still have made a good buy.

Too often, we get carried away with one side of an argument and fail to see the whole in its proper perspective.

> **When a customer says your price is too high, he means he doesn't have enough information to justify the product being worth the price you are asking.**

So always think of your price relative to what the product will do for the customer. Customers measure the value of your product exclusively on that basis. When they look at a piece of furniture and they see it as only a sofa and they don't see all of the things it can and will do for them when they own it, then your price *is* too high.

A salesperson exists at all only because the information the customer needs to understand fully the benefits of a product is not self-

BENEFITS   BENEFITS   BENEFITS   BENEFITS

evident in the product itself. If a salesperson doesn't have that
▶ information and can't supply it, then he has failed in his main
function.

When you have your five groups of knowledge, you are really
anxious to hear those words most feared by the order taker: "Your
▶ price is too high." These words tell you that the customer likes what
he sees. He wants it but you are going to tell him more about what it
will do for him before he will part with his money.

Most of the time, when you ask, "Mrs. Customer, are you saying
that this is the sofa you want and would buy if the price were not so
▶ high?" the answer is yes. Assuming your price is not negotiable, all
you have to do to answer that monster objection is go back in and
raise that pile of benefits.

In the case of the tires, you could have pointed out that the benefit
of the $100 steel radials was safety. But that benefit, if unexplained,
may still leave the price too high. When you point out how the
customer might feel should he take the cheaper tire and, God
forbid, have an accident that injured or took the life of a loved one,
then the picture painted in his mind is much more vivid and the
benefits of the steel radial go way, way up in value.

Now back to the sofa. Let's suppose that you had told the customer the sofa was easy to clean because the fabric was protected by
ScotchGard®. That's a wonderful benefit from a wonderful feature,
but I can assure you that when you demonstrate how ScotchGard®
repels liquids and soil, the value of that feature goes up several
hundred percent. We have already proved that demonstrating
ScotchGard's® protection adds $70 to the value of a sofa, haven't we?

When acrylic carpets first came out, they resembled wool so
closely that even experts could not tell one from the other. However,
there were still a lot of dyed-in-the-wool believers in wool as the only

choice for carpeting. Truthfully, I can say that I never lost a sale when the customer said, "If it is not 100% wool, I will never buy it." Back in the early days, carpet was still quite expensive, so the customers were usually 35 or older. Whenever a customer made that statement, I'd say, "You know, sir, you cannot tell, nor can an expert tell wool from acrylic. Acrylic is more color-fast. It is mildew proof, moth proof, and more crush proof than wool. Furthermore, acrylic will outwear wool. But sir, for only one other reason I would buy acrylic over wool, regardless of all of those wonderful benefits."

Then I'd look him right in the eye and say, "Sir, I have two daughters and no sons. You know, if one of those daughters were to present me with a grandson, it would be one of the greatest joys of my life. I can assure you I am looking forward to that as much as anything in this world.

"As I am sure that you are already aware, every year our children are developing more allergies, and wool is one of the biggest culprits. If there was one chance in a million that my little grandson might be allergic to wool and could not come into his grandfather's home, why, for that reason and that reason alone I would buy acrylic. It's non-allergenic on top of being superior to wool on all of those other counts."

How many times I have seen salespeople lose sales when a customer stubbornly said, "If it's not wool, I won't buy it." With all of the other benefits, the salesperson would say, "But sir, it's non-allergenic."

But the non-allergenic quality of acrylic carpets is *not* a benefit until you give the customer a real-life picture and then, my friend, there ceases to be an objection.

And suppose the customer's child or grandchild was allergic to wool. Who is at fault then? You are, if you knew why he should buy acrylic instead of wool and did not convince him to.

I tell this story because time vindicates the truth of my sales strategy. How much wool carpet is on the market today?

Now, you can see more clearly the interrelationship between

> Knowing your five groups of knowledge . . .
>
> demonstrating, illustrating, and painting mental pictures of benefits . . .
>
> and using them to graphically illustrate price vs. cost.

34

THE DIFFERENCE BETWEEN NO AND KNOW

In few other products is price so far out of proportion to cost as it is in a bedding purchase. Consider the fact that at least one-third of the customer's life will be spent in bed. Physically and mentally that is the most important one-third of the customer's life. A promotional sleep set priced at $500 with a five-year warranty costs him $100 a year. A top-of-the-line orthopedic-type sleep set priced at $750 with a 15-year guarantee costs him $50 a year. Incredibly, the sleep set that costs $100 a year cannot possibly offer the orthopedic support and quality of sleep that he will enjoy with the sleep set that costs $50 a year. But even more important, if he sleeps better, he works better, he feels better and he's a better husband, father and person. Bedding is an excellent example of an area where your ability to explore benefits is of paramount importance, but product knowledge is always important.

One danger in perfecting your selling skills in bedding is that the sales become so easy you'll want to spend all your time there. On large furniture showroom floors where customers and salespeople are free to roam, it is not uncommon to find one or two salespeople who account for a very high percentage of the company's total bedding sales.

The reason I call this a danger is that it does not give you the total earning capability of the entire floor and success in just one area tends to make a salesperson lazy when it comes to staying current on the five groups of knowledge.

The other day, my 11-year-old Carey and I were on the practice tee at the country club. She said she wasn't going to hit her five iron. I asked why. She replied: "Because I just can't seem to hit it. I am hitting my five wood real well and my eight iron real well so I am going to practice them."

I said, "That's great, but when you play, what are you going to do when you have a five iron shot? As a matter of fact, the five iron is the very club you should be practicing with. When you see a pro practicing after his round during a tournament, you can bet he is practicing those shots he was having trouble with."

A bedding customer should be considered one of the prospects for additional items. I find the salespeople who gravitate to one department will not be top producers because they do not learn to handle add-on business. I personally have sold hundreds of new bedroom groups to customers who were about to buy standard size bedding because their bedroom suite had a standard size bed. Once I convinced the man and woman that they were going to get a better night's sleep on a king size sleep set and told them that we had a sale on our bedroom groups with king or queen size head boards, it would amaze you how many customers about to spend $300 or $400 on a regular size sleep set would wind up spending $2000 to $3000.

Like all professions, selling is a growing experience. When you take the easiest route, it leads invariably to a dead end.

You Will Not Change the Customer's Mind

This will be hard for many of you to accept at first, but if you are going to become truly professional, it's a critical point.

You have heard it said forever: The customer is always right, Never argue with a customer. The list of similar maxims goes on.

Then you read books on selling that tell you that you must overcome customers' objections. Many salespeople find this a contradiction and, of course, they have a ready excuse not to develop techniques because they say you never argue with customers and therefore you accept their reason for not buying. Thinking like that can cut your income in half.

Let's see where the confusion comes in and how you can cope with it. There are five basic reasons a customer will not buy from you:

They have no need for your product or service.

They have no money.

They are in no hurry to enjoy the benefits.

They have no desire to own.

They have no trust in you.

For our purposes, we want to establish these five issues to make a very important point that will vitally affect your sales career. Because you will hear customers say, "I do not need it" and still make the sale.

Or "I do not have the money," and still you will make the sale.

"We are going to wait until you have a sale," or "I'll wait until your new models come in," — in these and a thousand other ways they will plainly state they are going to wait — and you will still make the sale. They will say, "I do not want it" — and you will still make the sale.

Or "I do not trust you or your company to live up to your promises" — and you will still make the sale.

Here's how you will overcome these objections. When they flat out state they are not going to buy for one or more of these reasons, you will understand that you will never get them to change their minds.

That's right! Understanding this will make the difference in getting the sale much of the time.

You might reasonably ask here, "If they say they don't have any money and I can't get them to change their minds, if they say they don't like it, how am I going to make the sale?"

Understanding why they object will actually help you understand how the sale is made and in fact they will not have changed their minds at all. Every one of these objections is the customer's way of saying, *"No. I will not buy your product for this reason based on what I know about your product at this time."*

What they are saying is "If you *cannot* give me more information, my answer is no." When you give them more information and they *know* more, they don't change their minds. In fact, they say, "Oh! that puts a different light on it. Now that I know that, I will take it."

They have not changed their minds. They have made an entirely new decision . . . with your help.

But if you took away the new information and asked for their decision, you'd be right back where you started. The answer would be no.

Now, this might sound contradictory, but let me illustrate.

> LADY LOOKING AT A SOFA: I like that. How much is it?
> SALESPERSON: It's on sale for $800.
> LADY: No, I don't like it for $800. That's way too much.

The sofa had been custom-ordered for the governor's mansion at a cost of $1,600. The governor had made an $800 deposit. Because it was for the governor's mansion, the factory had added a good many very expensive features as a courtesy to the governor and for the prestige they would derive from being able to say their sofa was in the governor's mansion. Before the sofa arrived, the governor was voted out and the new governor had gotten in on promises of austerity, pointing to the extravagance of the former governor and naming the $1,600 sofa as an example. Because the order had been canceled and the $800 deposit held, the company was willing to sell the sofa for the balance due — $800.

Can you imagine how easy the sale would have been had you pointed out these facts to that customer? She could easily reassess that sofa with your new information and make a new decision, couldn't she?

Too often, the salesperson tends to take offense at a customer's objection because of what the salesperson already knows. This is another reason why so many sales are lost.

Whenever the salesperson tries to prove the customer wrong, the old adage is proven one more time: The customer is always right. She knows what she thinks, based on the information she has, and at that point her opinion is correct. It is up to you to supply the additional information she needs to reassess the situation and make a new decision.

When she said she liked the sofa and asked the price, she had already made a decision. When she got the price of $800, her response was "I don't like it at $800."

With new information (the price) she made a new decision. *She had not changed her mind.*

If you asked her at that point if she'd like it if it cost $200, you can bet your bottom dollar she'd say, "Of course." Salespeople who are weak accept the customer's opinion that the price is too high and lose the sale. They also lose confidence in the value of the product. When confidence goes, enthusiasm follows. Once more, new information would have caused that customer to reassess the sofa and make a new decision.

The spendthrift governor's sofa is an imaginary situation I created just to make this very, very important point:

"NO" only means "I don't KNOW enough."

Whether you are new in sales or have been in sales for years, when you learn the difference between NO and KNOW and do something about it, your career will take on an entirely new and exciting dimension. On top of that, you are going to make a lot more money. (Note: Many examples given in this book assume you have failed to execute properly some phase of your sale. That's why the objection came up when it did in your sales presentation. The examples serve to demonstrate how you can still get the sale, although it may be harder.)

35

Phase Four: Presenting

WRITING THE ORDER

C an you imagine a sale lost because the salesperson wasn't ready when the customer said yes? I've seen it happen hundreds and hundreds of times. Not being ready at that critical time indicates other weaknesses, but for our purposes we want to address this subject right now.

If you go to any large furniture store today and do a little eaves-dropping, I guarantee you will see customers who have said yes sitting in the lounge by themselves. You will see customers sitting on sofas and chairs they have said they would take and there is no salesperson present. You will find entire families gathered around a dining room group, their decision to buy already made, and the salesperson nowhere to be seen. You will find couples in closing booths who are committed to buying but the salesperson is missing.

And where are these salespeople at this most critical time? Running all over the store, getting ready to write the order.

Looking for sold tags.

Looking for an order book.

Looking for a ball point pen.

Looking for a calculator.

Looking for a delivery schedule.

Looking for a credit book.

Running from item to item, listing it on a tablet.

> **When you are forced to leave a customer for any reason during a sale, you give up control of the selling situation.**

You have left them to discussions which you will not hear and perhaps to voice objections that you will never have a chance to respond to.

If you leave after the customers decide on a certain group, they may discuss other groups, causing them to question their decision. When you return, at best you may waste more valuable time getting them back to their original decision. In many cases, because you weren't privy to their reasons for a change of mind, they are out the door before you know what hit you.

This can also happen when you interrupt your presentation because you don't have all the information you need to answer the customer's questions. By the time you return, they have moved on to another area in the store and have forgotten the group or item you left to get more information about.

This kind of performance will cost you sales. If it happens often, you are going to lose *a lot* of sales. Frequent sales losses are a symptom of your lack of diligence in having your five groups of knowledge up-to-date.

It is tragic that a customer's problems should go unsolved because of a salesperson's sloth. The salesperson who loses a sale after the customer has said "I'll take it," cannot be forgiven if the loss was due to negligence.

I hesitate to make this next statement because it leaves a way out for those weak salespeople who do not want to assume responsibility for their own faults.

Under the best conditions, in the best-run companies, every salesperson is going to have to leave his or her customer unattended at times for any number of reasons. These absences the salesperson can't control can make the sale extremely difficult.

The major goal of this book is to get you each and every sale that you should be getting right now and then to help you get more and more sales as you mature and develop your knowledge and skills. That goal will never be reached if you take lightly those basics from which all of your sales will come.

Absence is one of those basics.

No retail company is likely to subscribe to everything this book proposes, and many could conflict with my proposal because of their control systems and the way they process paperwork, but the principle is sound and the sales lost will continue if you do not develop more ways to stay with your customer throughout the entire sale, avoiding those distracting things that take you away.

Start with phone calls.

No outside factor is more disturbing to a sale than a salesperson leaving to answer a phone call. Just think back over the times when you were a customer and a salesperson excused himself to take a call.

How many times have you been in a restaurant when, just as you laid your money and check on the counter, the phone rang, the cashier picked it up without saying one word to you and then proceeded to have a long conversation while you stood there completely ignored?

Remember this: your customer feels he has seen everything you have to offer once he has walked though your store and looked at the price tags. You know and I know that little, if any, value was established on that walk-through because he had not determined what he needed and none of the wonderful and exciting benefits of your products had been explained or demonstrated to him. When you get back from that phone call, the customer may already have left or, if he is polite, may only be waiting to say he looked at everything and didn't see anything he wanted.

Now, how important was that phone call?

When I was a boy, we had a family doctor who was a good friend of my parents. I remember him telling my parents that in more than 30 years of medical practice, he had received hundreds and hundreds of emergency calls, yet after all those years, not one had ever turned out to be a situation where he could have affected the outcome by rushing to the scene. I've thought about his statement for over 40 years and even as I write now, I recall how it affected me when I first heard it.

You will get phone calls that absolutely require your immediate attention, but they will be very rare. No professional, in any field, drops whatever he or she is doing to take phone calls. They have the operator take the call, get all the pertinent information, and advise the caller the call will be returned as soon as possible. You might lose a sale with this system, but it will be an exception and chances are that, as with our family doctor, rushing to the phone would not have changed anything. So, get your priorities straight. That customer standing in front of you right now is the most important thing in your world. Short of a family emergency that threatens one of your loved ones, nothing should distract you from your professional responsibility toward that customer and his problems.

There are other distractions, too.

Sold tags are covered in another part of the book, but sales orders are not.

If you work for a company by the hour, and they use a time clock to keep track of your hours, you are required to punch in and out and failure to do so can cost you money or even get you fired. As a commissioned salesperson, your time card or pay voucher is your order form. Your commission will be paid when the sale is completed according to company policy.

Some companies use a control sales ticket and only issue them when you come to the counter to write up your sale. In that case, you should get an order form book from an office supply store so you can follow this method.

A short note. Many books I have read on selling advise you to hide your order form or contract from the customer and to refer to it only as paperwork. I find no fault with this, except that it avoids the issue. My own experience is that the most truthful approach is always the easiest and quickest. For example, when I'm showing a product to a customer and he asks the price, I like to list it on a purchase order along with all of the item identification numbers right then and total it up, even including the tax and any other charges. Then, if the customer goes ahead with the purchase, all I need is his signature.

If he changes his mind and chooses something else, the worst that can happen is I have to throw away that ticket.

Once in awhile, when you step up to the item and start writing information on a sales order form, the customer will say, "Hey, wait a minute. I only asked the price! What are you doing?"

You simply say, "I am only listing the items that you've expressed an interest in. Should you decide to buy them, I find this saves my customers a lot of time — which they all appreciate. If they don't buy, all I have to do is tear it out and give them a copy so they can take it with them to compare as they shop around."

When you make your notes on an order form instead of a scratch pad or tablet they do not have to be rewritten onto an order form if the customer does buy and you decrease the chance of making a clerical error. You also save valuable time and you stay right with the customer in the most critical moments of the sale.

When you have the order form all filled out, all you have to do is say, "Mr. and Mrs. Customer, if you will just put your O.K. right there, I can get your order processed right away."

More important, if the customers don't buy, you still have their full name, address, phone number, delivery instructions, and any other information you need. So write that order completely.

When they get ready to leave, you say, "Mr. and Mrs. Customer, if you do decide to go ahead with the purchase, all you need to do is call me and everything will be ready to go. I find I eliminate mistakes and make happy customers by doing this." If your company requires that they come in to complete the purchase, you say, "Mr. and Mrs. Customer, should you decide to go ahead, all you need to do is bring this to the office and your order will be processed immediately."

When your customer comes back with a fully completed order form with your name on it, there is never a question about who made the sale and who gets the commission.

The benefits of this method are endless. Besides, you have all the information for a follow-up call if they are not back right away.

After he has tried every close he can think of and the customers still leave without buying, the true professional thinks of some legitimate reason to call them later with more information so even if they have placed an order elsewhere, they may change their minds and still buy from him.

After all, if you have invested time in that sale you should make every effort to get paid for it, don't you agree?

A few other reminders about staying with your customer. Have with you all the tools you need at all times. Tape measure, pocket calculator, more than one pen, sold tags (be an optimist — have plenty), and your order forms.

Remember, you are going to write an order for every customer you wait on. As a salesperson, can you imagine anything more exciting than that? I can think of only one — getting their signatures on that order.

The salesperson who writes an order for every customer he waits on will wind up with far more signed orders than the salesperson who doesn't start writing until the customer says yes.

If, as some sales teachers say, the order form poses a threat or causes fear in the customer, the worst time in the world to whip it out and have to explain it is while you are trying to fill it out after they have said yes.

> **If you're using a system that works for you and never poses a problem in making the sale, stick with it.**

The systems I recommend in this book are for the new salesperson or for those who are taking an inventory of their place in selling. Analyze your skills, your knowledge, and your results, then take an accurate count of every customer you wait on. If you are not closing at least 50% of them, your career is in trouble. When you are closing 70% you are cruising. Close 85% day in and day out, you are entitled to be called a master.

But not one percentage point before.

Here is a special note: The topic of the next two chapters — closing — actually has little importance in the daily life of the professional salesperson. Every top money earner I interviewed, when asked how he or she closed a sale, simply shrugged and said, "I just write it up, why?" Believe me when I tell you that's all there is to closing the sale — that is, *if* you have qualified your customer's needs and presented your product in a way that proves it to be the best solution to those needs. It is also true, however, that a real professional will not lose a sale for want of a good closing technique. Because of this, many of the best will average near 100% sales on qualified customer problems.

36

Phase Five: Closing

ASK FOR THE ORDER — GET THE SALE

I always have had a very difficult time with the phrase "closing the sale." Although all salespeople use the term "close" for getting the order and completing the sale, I believe the word is very misleading.

The dictionary gives 39 different definitions for "close." The one that comes closest to what we mean when we refer to closing the sale is: "to bring to an end; terminate." Only an order taker actually closes a sale by that definition. Professionals create customers for life. Their extra service on the first sale pays lifelong dividends. Even if their product is a one-time purchase, professionals expect to get sales through the recommendations of their satisfied customers.

A poor salesman is like a vending machine. It takes your money, thus terminating the sale. If it fails to deliver the product you paid for, that's tough. If it delivers the wrong product, that's tough. If you are not satisfied with the product it delivers, that's tough.

The vending machine closes the sale, all right. It takes the customer's money. And whether it dispenses the product or not, the sale is terminated. But it is not necessarily successful.

The only successful sale is one that winds up with a satisfied customer.

So let's define a successful sale as "a satisfied customer." That's it! When the customer is enjoying the promised benefits of your product, when he can logically justify his buying decision (though it was based on emotions) and has discovered that the benefits of your product far outweigh the price he paid — then, and only then, do you have a satisfied customer. Until he is satisfied with his buying decision, you do not have a successful sale.

The real proof of a satisfied customer comes when he is getting the approval of all those whose approval is important to him. That's when he starts telling other people about you and your product.

Only when you have completed a successful sale does the customer want to be your customer for life. Your only task after a successful sale is to ask the customer to be your customer for life and occasionally to remind him of your continuing interest. When you were trying to make the sale, you had nothing but good things to say to him. Now he asks: "Do you love me, or do you not? You told me once but I forgot."

None of this matters if you don't get the sale. And none of it happens if the product you sold didn't meet his needs or if you did not present and demonstrate the features that would be required to logically support his buying decision after his purchase. That's why I avoided dealing with the close until all the other phases of the sale could be covered and their importance established. To me, closing is exactly like sewing up the incision after a successful operation. If the patient died on the operating table, closing the incision is pointless. If you closed the incision before the operation was over, chances were the patient died.

Sears, Roebuck & Co., the world's largest retailer, was built on two mottos: "satisfaction guaranteed" and "we service what we sell." At any given time during Sears' long history, you might have purchased as good or better a product at a better price than Sears offered, but their customers stayed Sears customers because they were satisfied with the benefits and service they received.

THE PROFESSIONAL SALESPERSON KNOWS HE IS THE KEY TO A SATISFIED CUSTOMER

The professional knows the customer made the buying decision because of him and he is not only proud of it, but feels responsible for the consequences of that decision. He knows it is his responsibility to follow up on that sale and to be sure he has a satisfied customer. Because he does that, he — like Sears — makes that customer his for life.

All this preamble is designed to get the closing phase of the sale into a more appropriate perspective.

More damage is done to the selling profession and to the reputation of the retail trade by techniques and tactics sometimes used in closing than by all the other weaknesses of the profession combined.

Many books I have read on the subject of closing the sale refer to "the final objection," "the big one," and even "the price" (as though price were the biggest problem in selling). No top professional salesperson I interviewed felt that either price or closing was the ultimate problem.

Price is only a problem as it relates to the customer's budget or credit capabilities and far too many salespeople ignore those factors. When your customer does not buy because of price and there were features and benefits you did not present to him, then the failure is yours. The more benefits you demonstrate and describe, the less chance you'll have of hearing an item is "too" expensive when you start to close.

For now, let's assume you have done a good job of qualifying your customer and selecting the right product to meet his need. You are making the presentation.

So when do you try to close the sale?

At the very first opportunity you get! Just don't assume that writing the order and getting the money completes the sale. It does not.

Still, the sooner you get that buying decision and have the order written, the sooner you can get on with making the customer yours for life by searching out other needs that he or she has now or may have in the future.

HOW DO YOU ASK FOR A SALE WHILE YOU ARE MAKING A PRESENTATION?

Once it is apparent that your customer likes the product you have helped him select, he is ready to buy as soon as two things happen:
1. His need is met.
2. Promised benefits exceed the price.

If you ask for the order before this you will see why most books on closing say that when you get down to the final objection in a sale, "it is always the price."

To try to close before you have established how the product will satisfy the customer's need would be foolish. For example, the customer needs a sofa and you try to sell her a chair. Or, the customer needs an Early American sofa. You try to sell her a sale-priced contemporary sofa. The customer has a big family and needs a station wagon, and you try to sell her a two-door sports car.

Not even the novice would do those things, because they are obvious exaggerations of needs and attempted solutions. When and only when you have established your product as basically meeting the customer's needs or wants, then you must present the benefits of that product until they exceed — in the customer's mind — the price you are asking. When that happens, you should go straight for the close. Once these three things happen you'll get the sale.

How will you know this has happened?

You won't! Unless the customer interrupts your presentation and says, "I'll take it." In that case, write the order right then, but be aware that you have experienced an exception to the norm.

The rule is you are going to have to ask for the order to get it. And rarely are you guaranteed knowing exactly when to ask. Ask for the order as soon as the benefits exceed the price in the customer's mind. But since you have no way of knowing when this has happened, ask for the order by posing questions that will *not* get you a no, and start asking those questions as early as possible.

How early?

Again, an extreme example. As Mrs. Jones enters the store the professional salesperson greets her.

> MRS. JONES: I want to see that dining room group you have on sale.
>
> SALESPERSON: The one in today's paper?
>
> MRS. JONES: Yes, the one that was $999. I think I looked at it when it was $1,299.
>
> SALESPERSON: Was the $1,299 group the one you wanted for your home?"
>
> MRS. JONES: If it's the same one — yes. (They walk toward the dining room group department.)

SALESPERSON: If it is, will you need it right away?

MRS. JONES: Yes, we hope to have it for this weekend.

This sale is going straight toward the close. No feature benefit presentation is being made. As long as we are in a closing sequence, we pursue it until we hit an objection or until the order is written.

Note: I have over-simplified by omitting the fact that this was obviously a customer who had been waited on without buying. Any real professional would have asked her if another salesperson had waited on her before. I also omitted stopping at two other groups on the way to the requested group, inasmuch as that no doubt happened during her first visit.

So we continue our sale.

This closing should become easy for you to determine as you either have a customer who has decided on a product, or you don't.

If the customer has made up her mind before she comes in, as in the case of Mrs. Jones, then start a closing sequence as soon as successful communication is established. Caution! This is when you can talk yourself right out of an order if you don't take first things first. All the excitement and the fear of buying is still present until the final buying decision is made. When that decision is made and the order is written, then additional features and benefits reinforce it. (More to come on this subject in the chapter entitled, "Saying Goodbye.")

The fear of disapproval of a buying decision still exists if the customer is not willing to say yes, so the professional salesperson probes constantly with the right kind of questions during his presentation to move for the order.

A few more extreme cases.

A customer comes in asking for a specific advertised item and wants to see it quickly. Upon seeing it, he says, "I want it, I'm in a hurry." Then he pays for it and rushes out.

Another customer comes in and finds an item she likes. She takes hours trying to decide whether to go ahead or not and leaves without having bought regardless of any closing techniques used by the salesperson. She returns in a day or two and starts agonizing over her decision, sometimes taking eight to ten hours, and she still can't decide. This can continue for days, weeks, and even months.

All other buying decisions lie somewhere between these two extremes.

During my sales career, I have dealt with thousands of customers in a hurry. Of course, customers in a hurry pose no problem to closing the sale. We will deal with them later.

The customer who cannot make a decision and actually agonizes for days over the decision may have a mental illness. In over thirty-five years of selling I could count these on my fingers. You have no solution for them but then they are so rare as to hardly bear consideration.

When your customers are properly qualified, when you have helped select the right product and have made an informative presentation and demonstration of your product that got your customer involved, the great majority of those customers need almost no closing. Yet, one way or another you still must ask for and get the order before the sale can continue.

Top salespeople I interviewed confirmed this. If they lacked techniques they were usually closing techniques. They were excellent at greeting, qualifying, selecting and presenting. They really had little *need* for a lot of closing techniques, and certainly not for a lot of complicated, tricky ones.

EVEN THE MOST THOROUGHLY SOLD CUSTOMER WILL PROCRASTINATE

Your job is to help your customer say yes just as much as it is your job to help him select the best product to meet his need. A doctor's job is to convince you to have the surgery once he has determined that if your life is to be spared, you need it.

When the salesperson has determined the customer's need and found a solution for it, his job is to convince the customer to make the buying decision. The professional who has reached this point in the sale never gives up. Once he knows the customer's need and is convinced he has a solution to it, he does not stop until he has the order.

You can buy more books that contain more discussion about closing a sale than you can about all the other elements of selling combined, but the truth of the matter is that on any given sale, *rarely are more than one or two closing techniques usually needed.*

The problem is which of several to use.

As with product knowledge, once you have determined which product best meets the customer's needs, only the product knowledge necessary to sell that one item is called for. And most other product knowledge you have at that time is of little or no value.

After a sale is made, you start all over with a new customer, new needs, and knowledge of a different product that will solve a different set of customer problems. That's why you need to know about all of your products and why *you need a variety of closing techniques* to meet various situations.

> **You must know your and your competitors' products just as you must know inventories, advertising, finance plans, and store policies. You must have the same expertise in greeting, qualifying, and selecting. When you do, your presentation and demonstration *is* the sale. Only then does the closing technique become all-important. What a waste of effort if after your masterful presentation you can't ask for and get the sale!**

> **Among the millions of words written on selling, there is one common agreement: most sales are lost because the salesperson never actually asked for the sale.**

Weak salespeople don't ask for the order. They let the customer procrastinate. When the customer says, "We want to think it over," or, "Let us talk about it," he really just needs to be told: "You like it. You want it. Why don't I just write it up for you?"

Think about that whenever you feel that this chapter on closing is too complicated or that you could never learn or practice all of the techniques. Most — not just some — of the sales in the world today are lost simply because *the salesperson did not ask for the order.*

During the 50s and 60s, one appliance retailer in Chicago dominated appliance sales. He used a system in which salespeople who couldn't get a sale turned the customer over to a closer and was reputed to have one of the greatest sales closers in the world of selling.

This man always stood barring the customer's exit. As each customer attempted to leave, he asked, "Did you find something you liked?" If the customer said no, he started qualifying. If the customer's answer was yes, he asked, "Did you buy it?" If the reply was no, he simply asked, "When did you want us to deliver it?"

He claimed that well over one-half of all customers told him and he simply sent them over to an order writer with no more conversation.

Imagine! Over half of the customers who were going out the door without buying stopped and bought with no further selling. Incredible? No. According to most authorities the number one reason for the loss of a sale is that no one asked the customer to go ahead and buy right now. Today. My lifetime in selling convinces me this is true.

> **Closing lesson number one? If all else fails before the customer walks out the door, at least ask him to buy now. Believe it or not, some will actually say yes. But when the customer says no, ask one simple question, Why?**

That's it — Why? When you get an answer to the Why? and you offer a solution to it and then ask for the sale again, chances are you will draw a yes.

But if you get a no, you still have one simple question to ask again.

That's it — "Why?" When you get an answer to that Why? and offer a solution to it, you proceed to ask for the sale again.

At this point it should be obvious that you are now doing what you should have done in the first place. You are trying at this late date to qualify and make a presentation. I call this dumb selling because it's harder and it's slower, but if you have failed to do what you should have done and you still want the sale, you continue with the only question to ask, Why?

The professional continues this question and answer routine until he or she gets a yes.

Simple, isn't it? No? Why?

37

Phase Five: Closing

CLOSING TECHNIQUES

Your ability to get the customer to buy *now* is what will determine your level of success (and income) in retail selling.

That emphasized "now" is the kicker. I don't want to sound jaded, nor do I want to imply that a customer will tell a bald-faced lie, but after over 35 years in business, I believe when a customer says, "I'll be back," the chances are something near 100% she won't. No professional salesperson will ever settle for that response.

Occasionally, there may be legitimate factors that preclude making the sale right now, and there may indeed be those customers who come back, but the professional salesperson always sells and closes as if there were no tomorrow. He is determined to get that sale now. *This determination and his well-prepared selling efforts inspire the occasional customer whom he fails to close the first time to actually come back.*

Thorough preparations provide the professional salesperson with a constant flow of call customers. A few are "be backs" who were not closed the first time, but most of them are customers coming back for additional purchases.

Not closing is the most common failing of weak salespeople. Not only do they walk most of their customers without ever asking for the order, but then they make excuses like "Oh, they are coming back" and "I refuse to be pushy." Sure, they get as many "be back" customers as the top salespeople — after all, about 80% of their customers leave without buying. Only about ten percent of the pros' customers leave without buying. (Remember, the professionals constitute less than one-fourth of all salespeople.)

Start out feeling you must get the sale right now or chances are you won't. As you study the closing strategies of great salespeople, one thing stands out: they have a "killer" instinct. They are going to get the sale *now*. Right now! That means each and every closing technique you learn and develop must have one objective — to get the customer to buy now!

BUT NOTICE — They are going to get it by using professional skills and knowledge to help their customer make the decision now — not by pressure or pushing.

THE ASSUMED CLOSE

Go into every sale assuming the customer will buy right now.

"Mrs. Jones, I know you want this dinette as soon as you can get it. Let me go back to the delivery department and see if I can get it on tomorrow's delivery schedule." If you have made a good presentation, you can always assume the customer will buy if you just go ahead.

"Mrs. Jones, if you will just approve this order, I can have your sofa to you on our next delivery truck."

"Just put your approval right here and you can be sleeping on your new mattress and box spring tonight."

▶ Believe it or not, simple closes work and they work almost every time for the professional who has done the rest of the selling job well.

 A lot of the books that deal with closing the sale contend most good salespeople average five or six closes per sale. They could not
▶ possibly be describing good salespeople. Only glaring weaknesses in all the other phases of the sale can result in a sale needing five or six closes.

But then, no sale should be lost because the salesperson failed to close, either.

You should have one close that you polish to perfection, which will get you the sale most of the time. It will probably be the one that assumes the customer is going to buy right now.

The worst thing that can happen when you make this type of close is that the customer will say, "Hold it, I want to think it over." You then ask, "Why?" And recap your presentation. If they still need to
▶ think it over it's because they need more information or a reinforcing of the information you have already given them. They are not

going to get that information at home thinking about it. They are going to get it from you right then or not at all.

> Accept this fact: the simple close that asks the customer to buy right now will get the sale most of the time when you have completed all other phases of the sale.

THE "YOU LOSE" CLOSE

Every salesperson knows that just as there are reasons for the customer to buy at all, there must also be reasons for the customer to buy right now. The stronger the reason, the more chance for a yes.

We call this urgency. Most good advertising, for example, urges you to take action right now, or you will miss out on the offer.

Many great salespeople understand the natural human fear of loss and use that to create urgency.

Only a small criminal element in the United States will threaten or commit violence to take another person's property illegally by force. Most Americans will resort to violence to protect what is theirs. This common fear of losing what we have is one of the most powerful human emotions. When understood by the skillful salesperson, therefore, it is a powerful tool.

If I called you at home at two a.m. and offered you $50 to get up and do a one-hour job for me, you might refuse with very strong language. But if I were your next-door neighbor and called you at two a.m. to tell you someone was stealing your garden hose, you'd leap out of bed and do almost anything to prevent the loss of that $10 hose — maybe even jeopardize your life.

Although the close technique that manipulates this emotion is probably the most abused of all, it is still one of the best when used with skill. "You can buy at this price today and save $200 *because* it's on sale.

"You will lose the $200 and your chance to buy at this price tomorrow *because* the sale will be over."

The technique requires that you use the word "lose" and emphasize it.

That's why the ad that ends a sale usually does more business than the ad that begins it. I have always been able to wind up a sale far stronger than it started.

> **Final Week** — Shop before you lose the chance to buy at these prices.
>
> **Final Three Days** — Come in now before you lose the chance to buy at these prices.
>
> **Final Day** — Tomorrow you will lose the chance to buy at these prices.
>
> **Sale Ends at Midnight** — We're open till 12:00 p.m. Don't lose the chance to buy at these prices.

You can feel the urgency as you read this, can't you? And as the threat of loss increases, the urgency increases. It is a powerful buying motivator, and can be the most powerful closing tool in your bag when the customer wants to put off his buying decision.

The simple close is "Walk out and you lose."

Very few people will volunteer to lose. Most say, "I don't want to lose. I will take it."

Build up a good inventory of "becauses" and this close can give you many sales that would have been lost to procrastination.

A few suggestions to start with: "The next shipment will be new models. Although there will be little if any change, the prices will be much higher." *You lose if you wait.*

"I read in this morning's paper that the cost of bulk nylon just went up 40%. I am sure our next shipment will be at a much higher price." *You lose if you wait.*

"Although the sale doesn't end until the end of the month, we are almost out of these. When they are gone, no more will be available at the sale price." *You lose if you wait.*

"This is the only one we have reduced. They marked it down because of the small flaw in the fabric on the back of the sofa. At this sale price, it is bound to sell soon. When it's gone, I would be surprised if you ever found one on sale again." *You lose if you wait.*

I am sure you get the idea. You can find dozens of "you lose if you wait" stories all over your store.

Remember: *no* close will work if you haven't made the customer want the product and convinced her the benefits far exceed the regular price. Then and only then does the threat of losing the chance to buy at your price become urgent.

In many sales situations this series of three questions can close the sale right now.

Can you see where this product would save you money?

Are you interested in saving money?

When do you think would be the best time to start saving money?

Can you see how this product would improve your health?

Are you interested in improving your health?

When do you think the time would be to start improving your health?

Can you see that this product would save you a lot of time?

Are you interested in saving time?

When do you think you should start saving time?

Can you see where this product would make your family happy?

Are you interested in making your family happy?

When would be the best time to start making your family happy?

Can you see where having these tires would make your car much safer for you and your family?

Are you interested in making your car safer for you and your family?

When do you think you should start making your car safer for you and your family?

These three questions force a decision, but if you have not completed all of the other phases of the sale, these questions can easily turn into a high pressure tactic and lose sales and customers.

I include this technique because it is so often taught in books and seminars. It is a great technique for all those who have mastered the five groups of knowledge and are highly skilled in all sales techniques.

When improperly used, it comes out, "If you don't take the deal today, I won't let you have it later."

"Mrs. Jones, can you see where this sale price on our washer will save you over $100, make washdays a lot easier and give your family cleaner, brighter clothes to wear?" The salesperson exudes confidence and sincerity.

"You are interested in money saved, easier washdays, and clothes that are brighter and cleaner than you were getting from your old washer, aren't you?

"When do you think you would like to start making your washdays ◄

easier, your clothes cleaner? The sooner the better, wouldn't you agree?" Let me write it up for you now so you won't lose the chance to save over $100 on the washer you really want."

Yes, when you apply these three questions to the product with sensitivity and confidence, they can be a very strong closing technique. Practice, practice, practice is the secret.

LAST GAS STATION FOR 200 MILES

One of my favorite closes has always been the "last one." After making my presentation on the last item in stock, I say, "I am going to put a sold tag on this group while we look at lamps because we don't want someone else to get it first, do we?" I proceed then to get the name, address, phone and delivery date from the customer to put on the sold tag. It works almost every time.

Another close that introduces urgency into the sale is the interruption of your presentation. Say you are showing a group and you can see your customer likes your selection. You know it will meet her needs and you are sure you can sell it to her. Once you're sure of this, say, "Would you excuse me a moment, Mrs. Jones? I know there have been some orders written on this group this morning. I'll just run back to the office and make sure there is enough stock to fill your order because the factory is now running over 90 days behind on orders." (See why it is important to know your inventory?)

Off you go to the office to verify stock, knowing that if Mrs. Jones didn't object, you have the sale. When you return, assure her that one is reserved for her. Continue your presentation, then ask when she would like it delivered. Monday? Or will she need it sooner?

"CUSTOMER CHOOSES THE CLOSE" CLOSE

Here is a very simple yet very effective close: "How do you want to pay, Mrs. Jones? Cash, check, credit card, or do you want to open a time payment account?" Isn't it terrible when she says, "Well, if it's not over $10,000, I will just write you a check." This happens to the salespeople who know their five groups of knowledge and who do a good job of greeting, qualifying, selecting, and presenting. They seldom have a difficult closing job. Be alert, though, as the customer's answer may hint you have more benefits to prove.

The "Ask for the Moon" Close

Another way many expert closers work is to ask for more and settle for less. It works on an old principle that even bums on the street use.

> PANHANDLER: Say buddy, could you spare a couple of dollars for a hot meal?
>
> VICTIM: Bug off, fella.
>
> PANHANDLER: Fella, would you at least let me have enough for a hot cup of coffee. I'm freezing out here and they let me sit inside while I drink it.

Here's how selling experts use that one. "Mrs. Jones, did you want to go ahead and get the matching buffet server while you are here, or should I just write up the dining room suite?" Believe me, it works — but you have to use it to make it work.

The "Take the Bull by the Horns" Close

One of the best salesmen I ever knew used this close. He would simply say, "Mrs. Jones, you are going to buy that sleep set because it is what you and Mr. Jones need to get a good night's sleep and I am going to write it up for you." It worked for him and made him comfortably well off. I have known few salespeople who had the personality for this close, though. If you think you do, try it.

The "Something for Nothing" Close

Most companies at one time or another will have a sale that includes a bonus offer. Closing experts call these "something for nothing" closes. They know that their entire greeting, qualification, selection, and presentation must be made without reference to the bonus, even though the customer is aware of it. In other words, for the bonus to be free or "something for nothing," the primary need must be met by the primary item and its benefit value must still exceed the price before the bonus is introduced. For example: Buy a lounge chair, get the ottoman free.

Buy a mattress, get the box spring for half price.
Buy a five-piece dinette, get two extra chairs free.
Buy any dining room suite, and get a free turkey.

I am taking time to explain this valuable close and how it works for two reasons: First, there will be many occasions when you have to use it because of a company offer; second, because when order takers use it, it's often a sure-fire sale killer. As in many other closes, there is a tendency to ruin the sale because the bonus was designed to be used only as an added incentive to buy now.

When a customer asks for the advertised chair, the order taker guides him straight to it, says "This is the chair, and if you buy today, you get the ottoman free." If this play fails to get the order without presenting further features and benefits, then the order taker loses the sale.

Even if you don't get the sale at this point and you must begin your presentation, at best your bonus has already been lumped into the price of the chair. If that's not enough, further qualifying determines that this chair's size, color, or style does not really meet the customer's needs. The chair that would meet the needs does not include a free ottoman and therefore it becomes a nearly impossible sale. The moral of this story is: No professional ever skips any phase of a sale. He always completes them in order and that's why he gets rich doing easy work.

Back to the "something for nothing" close. When the benefits of the sale chair have been proven to meet the customer's needs and to exceed in value the price asked, then the ottoman is indeed "free." And your "one day only," "limited time," or "while they last" makes it so urgent that Mrs. Jones acts without delay. You actually hurry along from that point, just to be sure she doesn't miss out and *lose* the opportunity to get the free bonus.

It's a guaranteed winner when you use it right.

THE "BELIEVE IT OR NOT" CLOSE

For consistency alone, no other closing technique will out-perform simply asking for the sale. If you don't believe me, would you believe the Bible? "Ask and it shall be given to you." (A little out of context, maybe, but true nevertheless.)

More salespeople use this close successfully than any other.

By all means, ask for the order, right at the time you make the selection. Then if the customer says yes, you have the sale. If he says no and you ask why, when he explains you will know what you need to do to make the sale. I repeat this close over and over because, believe it or not, the number one reason for not getting the sale is beating around the bush and not asking for the order in simple language.

This has been proven every time, whenever management has ordered salespeople to ask for the order or lose their jobs, sales have shot up from 25% to as much as 60%. Imagine your sales and income going up 25% to 60% just by asking in no uncertain terms for the order.

Wouldn't that be something?

Plus — here's a big free bonus for you — when you ask often for the order, you will get many more chances to practice your techniques for overcoming objections. As you get better and better, so will your sales. That's even better, isn't it?

THE "YOU WIN" CLOSE

The master of this technique can hold onto lots of sales that were on their way out the door.

I'll explain. It is human nature to want to help. The Bible tells us it is greater to give than to receive and psychiatrists have proven that we humans get more satisfaction from giving than we do from receiving. This concept is very difficult to comprehend for some people, but as a salesperson you must accept and learn to use it to get maximum return on your efforts.

The best time to cash in on this technique is when the customer has said he wants to think it over and is preparing to leave.

At first, the salesperson appears defeated and in a humbled manner leans back and says, "You know, Mr. and Mrs. Jones, I sure would appreciate it if you folks would give me that order before you leave." Now here is where you just shut up and wait for their answer. ◀ It is uncanny how many times they will go ahead and give you the order when you do this.

THE "REDUCE THE DIFFERENCE" CLOSE

I never used complicated closes, but I have seen some master salespeople use them to perfection and they are a thrill to watch. These require practice, but, for some, they come easily.

One is used to overcome a price objection. Here's how it works and no doubt you have seen it a thousand times in ads. It costs only one cent a night to sleep on this new sleep set. Or, it costs only $1.37 a day on our easy payment plan.

For instance, a customer may have found a group of your competitor's furniture she liked for $2,000. She likes a group at your store much better, but it costs $2,600.

> SALESPERSON: Mrs. Jones, you do like this group far better than XYZ's $2,000 group, don't you?
>
> CUSTOMER: Yes.
>
> SALESPERSON: Do you mind if I ask you how long you would expect this group to last in your home?
>
> CUSTOMER: I don't know, but a long time. It's so well made.
>
> SALESPERSON: Would you say over five years, Mrs. Jones?
>
> CUSTOMER: Oh I am sure it will last far longer than that.
>
> SALESPERSON: I agree, Mrs. Jones, but let's say you keep it only five years. That's sixty months, or about 1,800 days, which means that spending the $600 more for the furniture you really want would cost only 33 cents a day. Wouldn't you pay 33 cents a day to have this furniture in your home instead of the other group you have been looking at? Of course you would.
>
> CUSTOMER: When you put it that way, I guess it doesn't make much sense not to take this group, does it?
>
> SALESPERSON: I'll write it up for you.

It may sound corny, but in the hands of a skilled salesperson, that close gets results. Work on it, practice it. Remember your daily costs and you can figure them quickly:

$600 is 33 cents a day over five years.

$1,200 is 66 cents a day over five years.

$1,800 is still less than a dollar a day.

Remember, what you are trying to do is get the customer to pay the difference, not the full amount. She has already agreed she would spend $2,000. It's the $600 more she is objecting to.

Break that down to 33 cents a day and it ceases to be worth objecting to on a $2,600 purchase. I tell you it's dynamite! Practice it with your buddy. As it starts to come naturally, you won't be able to resist using it on your tough money customers and it will get you the sale most of the time.

THE WORLD'S MOST-USED, MOST-EFFECTIVE CLOSE

As I traveled the United States and Canada between early September and mid-December of 1986, I visited every audio equipment retailer I could find time for, a total of about 50 different showrooms, shopping for a sound system for my 14-year-old daughter. Most of the stores I visited were specialized and belonged to huge nationwide chains, but I also visited large department stores, several big retail chain outlets, and many heavily-promoted independents. I never spent less than a half-hour in a store and in some I spent over an hour. About 18 of these stores I visited more than once. A few I visited three or more times, asking for the same salesperson each time. I asked hundreds, perhaps thousands, of questions. On two occasions, I even took my daughter with me. In over 90 days and in over 50 stores, *not one time was I asked to buy before I left.*

I have heard it said all my life that 75% of the customers who do not buy say they were never asked to buy. This shopping experience drove home that point to me so graphically that never again will I doubt it. Although for the most part the salespeople had the answers to my questions, not once was an effective demonstration of benefits made to me. About half the salespeople turned on the set, tuned to a radio station. A few inserted and played a tape and some put on a compact disc. None did more than one of these things and most did nothing. Now, if you find that hard to believe, let me add something else: Not one time was I asked *one* question. I was not asked a single question in this entire shopping fiasco, not even at the store where I finally made the purchase (and I had shopped that order taker three times before I gave up and bought the set in order to have it in time for Christmas). Still, I can tell you that on several occasions had I been asked to buy, I would have.

Yes, at any given time you may need a few closing techniques, but nothing will get more sales than simply saying, "Why don't you just go ahead and give me the order?"

The "Scapegoat" Close to Use When It's the Money But It's Not the Money

Most sales training programs counsel that the final objection is money, and all you have to do is provide more information to overcome it.

Sometimes this is wrong, but it can be even more so when you are selling to the mass market.

When does the customer suggest money is the final objection even though that is not really what is keeping him from saying yes? When that customer has fear of disapproval of her buying decision for some other reason.

If a wife is very close to her family and her in-laws, their approval of her buying decision is a must. If she is afraid her buying decision will meet with disapproval from any of these people, chances are she will put it off no matter how good a value it is — unless she can find a scapegoat. And we all know who the scapegoat for the wife is, don't we? Why, it's the husband, right? Of course, turnabout is fair play, because the scapegoat for the husband is the wife.

When you're selling furniture, it is usually the wife who wants it, and her decision usually requires her husband's approval. So bear with me here.

The wife has had a long visit with her mother. She tells Mom how hard up they are for money. Seems like it gets harder to make ends meet every day, and so on . . .

Most wives in America today have their bad days when it all seems to come at once and when it does, they have to cry on somebody's shoulder. Mother's shoulder is best, but for want of a mother's shoulder, best friends will do.

When that same woman gets something new, though, who is the first person she wants to tell? Why, those closest to her, of course; those whose shoulders she has cried on. It's only fair that the ones who had to listen to the bad stuff get to be the ones who hear the good stuff first, right?

Wait, though, there's the catch, the reason is the money but it's not the money.

When is a wife most motivated to want something new? When she is blue, wouldn't you agree? She feels bad, so she heads out to shop for something new.

With your help, she has found just what she wants for her home. You have proved its value far beyond your price and it's a one-of-a-kind. If she doesn't buy right now, she loses the chance to buy it and she loses the savings it offered. Her husband has said it's her decision. You have exhausted every technique you know and you lose that sale for a reason she would never admit to you in a million years. Fear of disapproval.

How can she go home and call her mother or best friend and describe what an exciting new sofa she just bought without risking disapproval? Whether it's real or imaginary, that fear is an insurmountable problem and you will lose the sale if she must take sole responsibility for her decision. After all, she just told them how she couldn't pay her bills. Now, she wants their approval for going deeper into debt.

Here is where the professional shines!

And here is where that good ol' boy her mother did not think too much of comes to the rescue. He becomes the hero *and* the scapegoat for her decision.

She gets the sofa, she gets the approval of all those whose approval is important to her, and he gets the blame.

The professional rides to her rescue — with a question, of course, because we all agree we lead the customer to her decision with questions, don't we?

This may be the best of all closing questions: "Mrs. Jones, what is your husband getting you for (your birthday, anniversary, Valentine's Day, Mother's Day, Christmas, Easter, etc.)? There is bound to be some occasion to mark by buying your new sofa."

What happens next? When you mention birthday or anniversary, the wife is going to think, "George, my birthday was two months ago and you never bought me a thing!"

Or, "George, our anniversary is coming up in less than a month. I can't remember the last time you bought me an anniversary present. I want this new sofa for our anniversary." So of course, she gets it, and George gets the blame.

Now, she can't wait to tell everyone. Her conversations go like this: "Mama, I am so excited. You will never guess what George did! Well, you know he forgot my birthday and he felt so bad that he bought me that new sofa I really wanted. It's just beautiful. I told him we couldn't afford it, but he's just so sweet to me." And the story gets repeated over and over.

She gets a double whammy here because she gets the approval she needs for her new sofa and she gets to prove that her decision to marry George against her mother's wishes was a good decision after all. Her mother may still wonder but daughter got the sofa, you got the sale, and everyone but George's mother-in-law is happy.

You have probably lost many sales where all the customer needed for you to close was a scapegoat to take the responsibility for the decision. If you listen closely, all too often you will hear the husband volunteer. After all, he gets a bonus out of the deal. If she got the sofa for her birthday, what's he going to get for his? Like I say, all happy marriages travel on a two-way street.

The scapegoat is first cousin to the embarrassment close.

THE "EMBARRASSMENT" CLOSE

Some of the best closers I have known used this one almost exclusively. I've always chuckled and felt a little sense of satisfaction whenever I used it or saw it used by a true master.

As a furniture salesman, I've long felt that the greediest, most selfish category of person in America as a whole is the average American husband. All you have to do is look down any average American street in the average American neighborhood to see the evidence of the truth.

How many of the Jeeps, pickups, campers, motor homes, boats, camping trailers on that street do you think the woman of the house wanted to buy? How much of the family budget went toward paying for them?

Do you know that a major reason for a housewife's going to work is so that she can satisfy her desire for a well-furnished home? Instead, all too often what she earns goes toward living expenses, freeing the husband's income for payments on a newer boat, car, pickup, or camper while his wife takes the bus or rides to work in a carpool.

I have always taken every chance I got to embarrass that guy into buying whatever I could sell him for his wife and family. I took my greatest satisfaction in doing it when he couldn't afford it. Let him sell his camper, boat or pickup to make the payments. It's far more important to meet the needs of his family than to feed his male chauvinist ego.

Here's how it is done:

HUSBAND: I want to think it over.

PROFESSIONAL SALESPERSON: Pardon me, Mr. Jones, do you mind if I ask what kind of car you have and what year it is? (Of course, if you watched him pull up, you saw that it was three years old and in good shape.)

HUSBAND: 1981 Pontiac Grand Prix, why?

PROFESSIONAL SALESPERSON: You know how badly your wife wants this new furniture, don't you?

HUSBAND: So?

PROFESSIONAL SALESPERSON: You know, I'll bet that when you get home and talk this over, if it is a question of her getting this new furniture — which she dearly wants and your entire family needs and will benefit from having — or you getting a new car, which could be put off for another year or two, I bet she would say, 'Oh! Honey, I want you to have that new car. I can wait a little longer for the furniture.' Give or take a nickel, isn't that about the way it is, Mr. Jones? You can see how much she wants that new furniture, but even more than she wants the new furniture, she wants the assurance that you want her to have it. Why don't you just approve this order by putting your name right here?

I don't know how many times as he signed I have seen tears rolling down his wife's cheeks as she says, "Oh honey, are you really getting it for us?"

I guarantee you I felt good all over every time it happened and I don't mind saying that I usually had to turn my head because I got a tear in my eye, too.

When you believe in what you are doing and what you are selling, it is fun, exciting, rewarding and easy to practice these and other sales-getting techniques that get your customers involved with your furniture, which in turn gets them involved with the inside of their home — which might make their family one of those that stays together.

Cars, boats, campers, Jeeps, motorcycles, motor homes, and the like may put the husband's pride on display for the neighbors on the block, but fine furniture puts the family's pride inside the home — where it belongs. Yes, I believe in taking drastic action if it will strengthen the family bonds in this strife-torn world of broken homes and I am proud of my actions that move sales along in this manner.

I don't want to be known by any other name. I want to be known as John F. Lawhon — the seller of furniture who helped make happier homes.

But, the person selling life insurance, securities, automobiles, boats, clothes, homes, jewelry, furs, anything and everything sold today from pots and pans to private jet airplanes must passionately believe his customers are going to be better off when they are enjoying the benefits of his products. Those salespeople take great pride, too, in embarrassing a buyer into a decision that will get the customer involved in and enjoying those benefits. When you feel this way, the embarrassment close is a lot of fun.

If, as some believe, God has a calling for all people (work which He has chosen them to do) then I am glad mine was to be a salesman, because there is no higher calling in my mind.

I also love this high-paying, easy work. I hope everyone who reads this book will join me in this rewarding career and practice it to the maximum of their God-given talents.

Once you have digested where closing fits into the sale, then there are many good points for you to learn from books that teach closing techniques.

We have finished the closing phase of the sale. The sale is made. The case is closed.

Wrong!

The selling has just begun!

PROFESSIONALS KARATE THE SALE

Karate is based on the fact that the mind directs and controls every action taken by the body. The same was true, we found, with the Principle of Reflection.

If you attempt to break a two-by-four plank in half by hitting it with the side of your hand (as you've undoubtedly seen experts demonstrate on television) there is little chance you will break the board and a good chance you will break your hand no matter how strong you are or how hard you hit the board if you don't understand the *principle* of karate.

You determine that you want to break the board. Your mind programs your hand to hit the board and stop. Now, because when you hit the board on a practice try it hurt, chances are you *won't* be trying again but if you do, two things will happen: (1) your hand is going to hurt and (2) the board will remain unbroken.

To succeed in breaking the board you must first remove the board from your mind entirely, and concentrate on striking an imaginary object a foot or two beyond or beneath the board. Your mind must program your hand to hit with all your strength something that is well past the board. The result is that your hand will go through the board in its effort to strike that imaginary object.

A professional golfer who seems to swing with great ease can drive the ball 275 yards while a hacker swinging with all his might only hits his drive 200 yards. The professional's mind tells him or her to hit through the ball while the hacker's mind relays to his hands that he must hit the ball and stop. The secret of the professional's swing is follow-through.

You see, when the salesperson is only trying to get the sale, his mind has said, "Get the sale and stop." This is not different from trying to break the board with only a light blow after a painful and unsuccessful trial test. He can't bring himself to hit that board with all his might for fear of damaging his hand or suffering pain. Weak salespeople who try to get the sale and stop are the same way. They fail so many times that eventually they reach a point where they don't even try. They don't even ask for the order.

Selling is just like karate. When you are after a customer's business *from now on*, getting today's sale becomes easy — as easy as breaking a board for a karate master or making a 300-yard drive for a professional golfer.

> The secret of success in karate is follow-through.
> The secret of success in golf or baseball is follow-through.
> ▶ The secret of great success in selling is in follow-through.

It is a fact: Great salespeople never close a sale. They make sale after sale after sale to the same customers because they begin with their mind set on "karate-ing the sale." Their follow-through is what doubles, triples, and even quadruples their sales volume.

38

Phase Six: Saying Goodbye

SAYING GOODBYE

I f done correctly, saying goodbye to your customer makes the money roll in. You can leave many sales subject to cancellation and pass up one of your biggest sources of income if you fail to do two simple things when you tell the sold customer goodbye.

First, as you are saying goodbye and thanking your customer for buying, always reinforce the buying decision!

Before she bought, she questioned everything you told her because she knew you were trying to sell her something. *After she has bought, she still has those same fears and doubts. She bought because of what you told her and unless you reinforce her decision, as she drives home her fears return. She starts questioning whether or not some of the things you said were just to get her to buy.*

How many millions of sales are cancelled every year because of this phenomenon no one will ever know. Every authority I have discussed it with agrees it is a significant cause of cancellations. You can avoid it by reinforcing your customer's buying decision. Here is how.

GOOD BUY, MRS. JONES

Wait until your customer is all through with her purchase and is ready to leave the store.

As you prepare to say goodbye, thank her for the order, assuring her that her decision was a very good one. Many salespeople actually save a feature or two to use at this time.

"Mrs. Jones, you have certainly made a good decision — I think that sofa is one of the best values in the store. By the way, I forgot to point out one very important feature that makes it an even better buy. The sofa you chose has a thin foam padding on all of the edges and corners of the frame that prevents damage to the fabric should the sharp edge of the wood be bumped. It also gives your sofa a softer look. That's such an expensive feature, I don't know how I forgot it. That extra feature alone makes your good buy even better. I know you will come to love your sofa more, the longer you have it."

GIVING YOUR CUSTOMER YOUR CARD

"Mrs. Jones, I want you to have my card should you have any reason to call on us. If you do, please call me first." Never say "If you have any problem, call me first." Why plant a great big threatening cloud in her mind where none exists nor is likely to?

Now here is where you go for the plus business. During the sale, you have determined other needs Mrs. Jones has for her home. You always wait to address those until after her first need is met.

"Mrs. Jones, I like to let my customers know when we get new things they might need and like. Or, when we have something that is going on sale you might need. If it is a special sale and time is important, I'll call you, otherwise I'll just drop you a note.

"You've been such a pleasure to help and serve. You might have noticed that I gave you two of my business cards. If you have friends who need help with anything at all for their homes, please give them one of my cards. I'd love to help them any way I could. *And thank you. Thank you again for your business."*

Now you can easily see why you will want complete information on your business card. (See the chapter entitled "Your Business Card.")

No top salesperson to whom I talked failed even on the smallest purchase to thank the customer profusely and to reinforce her buying decision as she left the store. Not one of them failed to give her his card and ask for future business. But, here is where they started to miss out.

Time after time, my interviews revealed that salespeople who did the little things were most often the top-volume achievers in every company.

Even their thank-you cards made a difference. Two salespeople I interviewed sounded like perfect echoes of each other. Both were apparently executing every step of a sale with the same degree of professionalism, and both sent thank-you cards as a follow-up. So what was the difference?

The first salesperson averaged $80,000 a year in income. He sent thank-you notes to each customer he waited on whose name he could get whether he sold them or not.

Every note he sent out had a personal message besides saying thank you.

Mrs. Jones,

Thank you again for your recent purchase.
I will be watching for that kneehole desk you liked.
You can expect a call the minute one goes on sale.

Salesperson

The second salesperson averaged $56,000 a year in income. She sent thank-you notes only to each customer with whom she made a large sale. Every note she sent was a form letter furnished by the company and it read:

Thank you for letting me serve you.

Salesperson

These two great professionals worked on the same sales floor, yet he earned a third more than she. I found that among the top salespeople the only differences were in the little things, like offering two business cards instead of one and sending sincere thank-you notes that told the customer of their genuine interest. In the case above, the top earning professional made sure he sent thank-you cards even to those customers he *failed* to sell.

Here are some other excellent samples from winners:

Dear Mrs. Jones,

I was so glad you and your family were the ones who got the floral quilted sofa. It was such a good buy and your entire family seemed so excited about it. You all made my Friday for me.
I made a note about the bunk beds you will be

needing for your boys' room. The first time they are on sale, I will give you a ring.

Thanks again,

Salesperson

Dear Mrs. Jones,

I was so glad you and Mr. Jones decided to go ahead and get the premium sleep set. You were both so pleasant to help. I just felt better all day long.

Thank you so much,

Salesperson

P.S. You can bet I will be watching for that other blue velvet chair you needed. The minute I find one, I'll call, even if it's at another store!

Dear Mrs. Jones,

I am writing to tell you how much I enjoyed helping you yesterday. I felt terrible that I couldn't solve your problem. You were so pleasant, I really wanted you to be my customer.

I made a note of the recliner you wanted. I will be watching for it even though you may find another one in the meantime.

Also, I made a note about the king sleep set and you can bet the first time they are reduced in price, you will be the first to know.

I love selling furniture because I get to meet people like you.

Thank you,

Salesperson

Mrs. Jones,

Thank you and your family for letting me be a part of your family yesterday. You all were so excited about your new family room furniture, I felt as if I were getting it myself.

Again, let me say thanks.

Salesperson

P.S. The next time we have our dinettes on sale, yours will be the first family I call.

These examples should show how your sales can be multiplied. In every one of these notes, the customer was told to expect a call the minute a specific item arrived in which they had shown an interest.

Be Sure to Make That Follow-up Phone Call

Filing, writing, mailing and making the promised phone call will take you no more than five minutes a day and can almost guarantee you extra sales every time.

I interviewed so many salespeople who said, "I tried sending thank-you cards, but they took too much time." Others said, "I send cards to customers who make a big purchase." Still others said, "I know I should send thank-you cards but I just put it off."

I asked many of these same salespeople if they thought bitching was a good way to let off steam. They said yes and without further prompting started telling me all of the things wrong with their company, their merchandise and the other salespeople.

If they spent a fraction of their complaint time sending out sincere thank-you notes and following up with promised phone calls, they'd double their income.

If you are just going to send a printed form card from your company that says an insincere thank-you and has no personal touch, save the postage and don't bother. Hopefully, you *said* a sincere "thank you" when your customer left. Don't destroy the good you did then with a phony follow-up card.

A professional realizes that five minutes of his day

invested in personal thank-yous and follow-ups can
make the rest of the day more productive.

No company you work for is going to have a steady flow or surplus
of customers all the time. While you are waiting for a customer, you
aren't making money. Write your thank-you note as soon after the
sale as possible. The best salespeople kept note paper and envelopes
in their sales books and wrote them at the end of each sale as a part of
the sales process.

Suppose your two slowest days are Wednesday and Thursday.
During slack time on Monday and Tuesday, call those customers
you promised to call or who expect you to call to continue the sale.
Let them know the item is in, the sale is on, or, whatever you
promised to tell them and set up an appointment for Wednesday or
Thursday.

See how this could buy you a brand new Cadillac in a short period
of time? The only question you have is where and how you're going
to spend that short period. In the lounge with the losers? That gets
you nothing, except possibly fired.

Besides, sending thank-you cards and making phone calls makes
you feel good. There is no question that follow-up phone calls will
get you more sales when the right item at the right price comes
along.

You might tuck another business card into its own envelope, on
which you have had printed:

> Enclosed is my card. Should any of your friends be
> considering furniture, I would love to serve them, too.
>
> Thank you.

Even the one-out-of-a-hundred response can add up to thousands of dollars in commissions.

If you doubt the value of follow-ups, consider this: a four-year
national survey showed that 74% of the people who quit doing
business with a company did so because of indifference to the
customer by company employees.

*More important, the survey revealed that the average customer is going to
make at least one important furniture purchase every year.*

And all-important, as far as you are concerned, 47 out of every

100 furniture buyers made their purchase at the store where they had bought last.

> **Forty-seven out of every 100 customers you sell will return to your company within a year to make another purchase.**

That's why your thank-you card and phone call assures you of that sale. But if 47 return with or without a thank-you card, there is a very good chance that 70, 80, 90, even 100% will return to you within one year. They will bring other customers with them, if you send out sincere thank-you cards and show a continuing interest in your customers' needs.

When two salespeople with equal talents, equal knowledge and equal skills are selling side-by-side on the same showroom floor and do not have equal sales, the only question to ask is our old friend WHY?

Usually, there's only one answer: repeat business. It takes less than half as much time to make a second sale to a customer as it did to make the first one. A pre-schooler can figure out the result. More volume, less time.

So selling is easy, high-paying work, provided you invest an extra five minutes of your time in follow-up with every customer. At the end of every year, in good times and bad, when everybody else is moaning about bad business, yours will be booming. This step, along with "The Better Deal" (which you'll find out about in a later chapter) are the secrets of those giants of retail selling . . . and simple steps for making customers *yours* for life!

When you have enough of these loyal customers, you have a secure high income, because these people are *your customers*.

Phase Six: Continued

YOUR BUSINESS CARD

I have always been an early riser. I was one of the first to arrive every morning at any store, whether I managed it or owned it or just worked there. Over the years, I guess I've picked up or paid someone else to pick up hundreds of salespeoples' business cards that had been thrown on the parking lot.

Think about that. By nature, most people aren't litterbugs. For them to have been so dissatisfied with the salesperson who gave them their card that they could hardly wait to get outside and throw it away tells you a lot about that salesperson. I have even found cards the customer had not only thrown down but had ripped up and even ground underfoot.

I know you don't want that to happen to yours. *Your business card can and should be your most useful sales tool.*

You need a card that includes all the information your customer needs. The card should also have all of the information anyone might need who has gotten your card from a second party. (See "Saying Goodbye.")

I'd like to show you an ideal business card with all the information it should contain. If your company doesn't have a card with this information on it, show this chapter to your supervisor. If your company doesn't want to furnish the card, ask if you can have your own printed. Even if you must pay for them yourself, do it, it's a good investment. A good card is vital and it's loaded with information.

Your name must always be printed, not written in by hand, which suggests your presence is temporary. Your card must indicate permanence in order to instill customer confidence.

I recommend a folded card of the dimensions shown in the diagram.

YOUR NAME should be set in larger type than anything else and

Cherrywood Dinette & Barstool

The one place where you can choose from
600 barstools and 200 dinettes in stock.

Open daily 10-6,
M & Th 'til 8,
Sunday, 1-5.

Visa &
Mastercard
welcome.

MIKE O'GRADY

4340 S. Mango • SW corner of Cherrywood and Mango
PHONE: (212) 628-1209

_____

_____

_____

Financing Available.
We will gladly work by appointment.

should be centered. Obviously, the main reason you have a card is to get people to remember your name.

YOUR COMPANY NAME should appear with address, instructions on how to find your showroom if necessary, and phone number. This is *your* business card, *not* your company's card, even though it must be approved by your company. You don't care if they have ten stores in the city. Your card is designed to get that customer to *your* store to buy from *you*. If you did the selling job to get them to do that, then you must make it easy for them.

YOUR PHONE NUMBER. It is not a good idea to have your home phone number on your card. Many professionals prefer not to take calls at home. And, certainly, if you are willing to give your customer that privilege, you should get lots of credit from him for it. These extra services put your customer deep in your debt as you will see in the chapter entitled "Service Beyond the Call of Duty."

YOUR STORE HOURS. Many times your customer is excited about something you have shown her. When she gets home and starts telling her husband about your great value, his first comment is, "Well, they're closed by now." She needs an answer right then and chances are she has forgotten your store hours, so that information must be on your card.

YOUR CREDIT PLAN. The husband's second comment is usually, "We don't have an account there. They probably don't have terms." She needs to know *right then* what terms are available. Every credit plan you have — even a "30 or 90 days same as cash" offer.

VITAL INFORMATION. Your customer is more apt to keep your card if it has information on it that she needs. That's why you always leave a blank space in which you are going to write the measurements of the item she is considering or has bought or other things that might come up during the sale and which will cause her to keep your card. The extra space is also a place to write your home phone number if you want to give it to the customer. Directions to your store, what categories of products your company carries (brand names, too) should also be on your card.

When you give your card to someone who will pass it to someone else, you must be sure the third party has all the information they'd need, too.

Learning how to use a business card to your advantage begins with some lessons on how not to use it.

CUSTOMER: I want to think it over.

SALESPERSON: Fine. Here's my card. If you decide you want it, ask for me, but remember, it is the last one. So, don't blame me if you come back tomorrow and it's gone!

As I say, I have paid to have hundreds of business cards swept off parking lots and this is the attitude that put a lot of them there. One other thing: if and when that customer decides she wants the item, sometimes she'll request that the salesperson who gave her the card *not* wait on her. It is a common occurrence and the irate salesperson who sees "his" customer buying from another salesperson begins to shout, "thief!"

WHEN WEAK SALESPEOPLE HAVE SENT THEIR CUSTOMER OUT THE DOOR

Can't you hear it now as I have so many times before, directed to other losers in the lounge: "Boy, what an old bat! I hope somebody buys that chair today because I know she is coming back to buy it. Nothing would tickle me more than to tell her it's sold." His card, by the way, is hitting the parking lot even as he speaks.

No company today can afford to keep a salesperson with that attitude. And certainly no professional salesperson can afford such an attitude.

Granted, I have already stressed that you make the sale while the customer is in the store. Nevertheless, after every effort has failed, you still try everything you can to get that customer to come back and buy from you. This small effort accounts for three to ten percent of the sales by top-income salespeople. A business card with the proper information on it increases the percentages.

Some of the world's greatest salespeople have their pictures printed on their cards. It is a good idea for retail salespeople. You might consider having one side with your name and the other with your picture.

40

The Better Deal

"IF YOU COULD BUY . . ."

E arly in my sales career, it occurred to me that every shopper in a retail store could be sold. More than 35 years later, I am totally convinced of this fact. A professional salesperson can raise the buying priority level in the customer's mind and wind up with a sale almost every time. Let's look at a few examples of this principle in action — both honest and not-so-honest.

A 19-year-old once came to my sales floor right off the farm. Tall, a little awkward, and definitely down-home country, he discovered quickly this very principle. He had a way of saying a few words that consistently got a positive result.

He'd position himself on the aisle that led to the office in a large store I managed. There was a reasonably steady flow of customers into the office for any number of reasons.

Other salespeople waited up at the front for a customer who was interested in buying something. If the customers needed the credit, service, or employment offices, or if they had other questions, they were sent back to the office area. As these customers passed by, this fresh-off-the-farm beginner (who had one leg casually draped over a console TV set) would simply ask, "Pardon me, folks, but would you be interested in looking at a $599.95 color television today?"

He'd pause just long enough for the customer to start to respond. As they started to move their lips — but before a sound came out — he'd go on. "If you could buy it for $399?" Again, a pause. Then, when the customer's lips made the first hint of movement, he continued, "Aside from saving you 33.3% today, I could arrange it on an account with 36 months to pay. It's right over here. Let me show it to you."

I watched him do that hundreds of times and I was always astonished at how often the customer followed him to the color TV.

More amazing was that, almost without fail, if the customer followed him, the set was sold.

The secret that made this work for him, a secret so successful he never stood in line for a customer at the front doors, enabled him to stay in the top ten percent of a very large sales force.

His technique was one of the oldest sales secrets. I have shopped in the bazaars of Turkey, Cairo, Morocco, and many other ancient trading centers, and have watched it practiced with such skill as to make it something beautiful to witness. Sight-seeing tourists from the four corners of the world were lured into tiny ancient shops and sold on lugging home purchases that cost them thousands of dollars.

I used to walk down lower State Street in Chicago and watch the true masters of this art. The first time it was worked on me I walked out of a store I didn't think I had walked in, owning a new, light blue, double-breasted gabardine suit.

I have taken many friends to a space in the Chicago furniture mart that sold blankets to furniture dealers who had never carried blankets.

I love to shop the Mexican border towns because there this technique is practiced even by young boys and girls with great skill. The time my good friend bought a diamond wedding ring from a desperate father in Juarez was a remarkable exhibition of the technique.

A thief who used to ply his trade in Oklahoma City employed this ancient sales technique to sell what he was going to steal even before he stole it. Like all the great sales techniques, I've seen it used for good and evil, practiced by saints and sinners alike.

It can make you thousands of extra dollars every year if you practice it and master it. Did you notice that I said not just practice, but master? Many, many people in sales today enjoy extremely high incomes and this is the only sales strategy they use. Many who have mastered it don't even know another technique.

If I thought this would be the only technique you would master from this book, I'd hesitate to include it. I always felt the TV salesman to whom I referred earlier could have been great, but this technique came so easily to him he never bothered to develop his potential or to expand it with other solid efforts.

Okay, if I have your curiosity piqued sufficiently, I want your solemn promise to read very carefully and then to go back over the explanation I am about to give until you fully understand this psychological phenomenon and why it can result in sales almost every time when practiced with integrity and skill.

PONZI AND THE PONZI PRINCIPLE

Many years ago, a man named Ponzi came up with an investment scheme that reaped millions of dollars from poor immigrants in America. His scheme was so simple it worked almost for no reason other than its simplicity. Ponzi set up shop and said if they would invest their money with him, he would use it to leverage foreign currency. He promised to pay a 50% return on their money every 90 days.

A few cautious people invested and at the end of 90 days he paid them their accrued interest, which was 50% of their investment. Suddenly, word spread like wildfire and within weeks he was actually taking in truckloads of money and anyone who wanted to could get his money back with interest anytime.

Needless to say, Ponzi's scheme was a fraud. There was no dealing in foreign currency. Any money he paid out was simply investors' money, but his scheme continued to work as long as income exceeded outgo. When the bubble burst — as they all do — thousands of people were sadder, wiser and poorer. Ponzi's greatest achievement was to leave his name attached to that racket. Because it's so attractive to greedy people, we still see variations of it cropping up.

In the 1960s, a scheme based on the Ponzi Principle began in Tulsa, Oklahoma, promising enormous profits, plus near-impossible tax benefits. The plan was garbed in the glamorous clothing of the petroleum industry, and when its bubble burst, hundreds of millions of dollars in investors' money had vanished. These victims weren't unschooled immigrants; they were the nation's and the world's leading bankers, judges, lawyers, entertainers, giants of business and industry — household names everywhere.

The two crooked examples identify a basic weakness. It is human nature to want a better deal. The immigrants with their pennies to invest and the rich, great and famous with their millions were both susceptible to a "better deal." Properly presented, such a promised return could border on the absolutely ridiculous and still claim the money of sophisticated banks and investors.

All the Tulsa scheme needed was a few people who had invested and gotten the promised return to tell about their windfall to others who trusted them and as the second tier investors got their promised interest, they of course spread the word even further. The perpetrator of the fraud never had to describe it to anyone after the first two or three because those who were being duped did the explaining for him.

And oh, did the money roll in.

Both of these schemes were criminal frauds, but they define the psychology behind them.

"WORD OF MOUTH" IS THE BEST ADVERTISING

When your customer is excited about the value of her purchase from you, she is going to tell others. Word of mouth. Others want to share the same excitement your customer experienced and told them about.

Read Emerson's essay on "Compensation" and you will see how all things have equal potential for positive and negative results, for evil and good. This same principle used honorably is what sold the American way of life and inspired us to produce the greatest nation in the world.

We have succeeded in creating wants in the lives of a nation by raising buying priorities to motivate people to work, produce, create, originate, invent, build, and seek education in such a way as to have transformed the entire world. No promised miracles or prophecies of ancient soothsayers could ever have envisioned the transformation brought about by this sales-motivated society — all because deep down inside the soul of every human being there is the burning desire to get a better deal and ultimately to have a better life.

For a moment, let's backtrack to the young TV salesman. He used that same technique, discovering that if he could promise a deal on an item most people wanted and he could deliver the deal he promised, then he had a sale. All he had to do was practice the principle and the sales poured in.

A Bizarre Sale in Cairo

In the old bazaar in Cairo, Egypt, my wife and I were considering the most touristy of all tourist items — the handsome, full-length kaftan-like robes that both Egyptian men and women wear. We were admiring some particularly good-looking examples in one of the better shops when we commented to each other on how expensive they were. I heard a "pst, pst" sound and looking around saw an Egyptian man with his head sticking out of an alley way. He signaled me over. In broken English he asked if I like the robes. I said yes, but they were too expensive. He said, "How much you pay?" I said, "For those I wouldn't pay half of what they were asking." He said, "Sir, I can get you in the factory that made those robes and I can get you even better ones than those for less than half of those prices." I said, "Lead on." Well, down a narrow alley, up a crooked stair, through a couple of doors and — Eureka! — the factory.

We were shown the same robes we had seen in the shop and he quoted prices well under one-half those asked for the robes we had admired. Then we were shown some better versions we could buy at about one-half the price of the ones we had seen first. Then, using the most glorious of words, he took us into an inner room to see a pair that had been made up specially for the factory owner and his number one wife. The needlework and the rare one-of-a-kind fabric made up especially for the owner's own use was pointed out. Surely no finer garments existed in all of Cairo and should they be offered in the bazaar they would bring many, many times the price of the original robes we had seen.

Sadly, the owner's wife, upon seeing them, was thrown into terrible mourning because they reminded her of the robes their precious child had been wearing when Allah in his mercy had called him from this life. Inasmuch as we were from America and the owner's wife would never see them being worn, our host was willing to sacrifice them for a fraction of the fabric cost alone.

To shorten this beautiful and romantic story, at a little over double the original prices, we had found our better deal.

And what a deal! What a deal! We couldn't wait to get back home to find an occasion to wear them so we could hold our friends in raptured silence as we told the exciting story about our better deal.

Unfortunately, the glamour and excitement disappeared before we ever left Cairo. First, when we told some friends in Cairo about our deal, we were informed that the man in the alley was not only the owner of the shop, but of the factory. The shop was bait, and the price tags a setup. Horror of horrors, a little more shopping and we discovered our most exclusive and expensive of all fabrics in some pretty cheap shops — for a lot less than we had paid.

A FAMILIAR RING IN MEXICO

Now down to Mexico with my good friend. A man solicited our attention from around the corner on a side street. Tears running down his cheeks, he told us his desperately ill baby daughter was over 200 miles away in Cuernavaca, the bus ticket was $14 and his only possession was a solid gold wedding ring with four genuine diamonds in it. With this statement, he leaned professionally toward the plate glass window of the shop and, using the ring, made a scratch in the glass, explaining that this proved they were genuine diamonds, as only a genuine diamond could scratch plate glass.

Even though the ring was very, very valuable, he went on, and cherished by him (it was his wedding ring), to be able to see his baby girl once more before she died (at this point, tears were flowing again, except now it was his and ours) he would part with the ring for $14 — the price of the bus ticket home to his child. My friend whipped out the $14 and threw in an extra dollar for something to eat. With that, the man disappeared and we walked on to a restaurant for lunch. Once we were seated, I asked to see the ring and I took off my own diamond ring and tried scratching the diamonds in his ring. I not only scratched them, I powdered them and then scratched away the thin gold plating on the ring. He left it as a tip for the waitress. That salesman had chutzpah, though. As we were leaving the restaurant, he sidled up and asked if we would like his wife's matching ring for only $10.

What a deal!

THE THIEF IN OKLAHOMA CITY

There was a thief in Oklahoma City who went up and down Reno Street, stopping in the bars and slinking up to customers and owners alike, nudging them and saying, "Hey buddy, you want to buy a hot?" Which always brought the response: "A hot what?" He would then say, "You name it and I'll steal it." If they showed interest and named something they wanted and could agree on a price, in a very short time the thief would return with the item as ordered. He did a thriving business, even though all his products were stolen. He would walk up to complete strangers who had no intention of buying anything and he sold the majority of those he asked. Cameras, watches, televisions — like he said, "You name it, I steal it!" The point is they got in the market to buy right then, once they thought they could get a better deal. (The thief spent a lot of time in prison simply because it was hard for people to refuse an obviously better deal.)

WINDOW SHOPPING

Here's the true story of my blue suit and what a deal *it* was. To show how this works, look at a drawing of the store.

As I wandered along State Street in Chicago, looking in shop windows, I came to a men's clothing store and was drawn to a blue suit I could see through a window. While I was looking at it, the owner quietly slipped out the door, got between me and the sidewalk, and then said in a very excited manner: "You like that suit? Oh my, my, my. You're a 38 long? Yes, yes, yes." He repeated himself: "You're a 38 long?" "Uh . . . yes," I replied. "Oh my," he said, "are you in luck." "Why?" I asked. "A month ago," he said, "a young man exactly your size bought one of those suits. He made a large deposit and we tailored it beautifully to fit him. He has not come for it. Come on in. It's in the basement. If it fits you, I will give it to you for only the small balance left due."

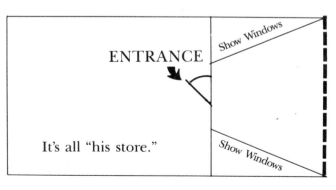

With that, he ushered me into the store and down into the basement. I waited in one room while he hunted in another. When he came out the suit was not the same and didn't fit. Oh, he felt so terrible. How could he ever make it up to me after wasting my time this way? And with that, he got a wonderful idea. He would have the beautiful light blue, all-wool hand-tailored gabardine double-breasted suit tailored to a perfect fit and sell it to me at a big discount.

After all, it was the least he could do.

Which is how I came to own a double-breasted, light blue, all-wool, gabardine suit and all I could say was "What a deal, what a deal!" I walked out of a store I never felt I had walked into. You see, I thought I was outside his shop on the sidewalk and only entered when I went through the doors. Not so, as far as he was concerned. I was in his store when I stepped off the sidewalk to look in the window. He made his sales working with people a weak salesperson would say were just window shopping. He knew when I stopped to look that I liked and wanted what I saw. All he needed to make a sale was a better deal.

A BLANKET DEAL

I especially admired a particular salesman I knew. Because few if any furniture dealers ever carried blankets, he'd have to be very lucky if he so much as found a person to talk to at the Chicago Furniture Market. But someone to talk to was all Nathan ever needed to make a sale, and a big one at that.

I can close my eyes and hear his beautiful selling words as clear as they were the first time I slowed down at the entrance to his space.

He started without preamble or introduction, woefully telling how his line was so hot and his customers in fine furniture stores were selling his blankets so fast he was completely sold out for the entire coming year.

With that, he magically produced a very large sign to which he had signed his name. It read:

SORRY, THIS SPACE SOLD OUT THROUGH
JANUARY OF NEXT YEAR. I WILL SEE YOU AT
THE JANUARY MARKET.

"See, I had this sign made and was not coming to market because I have nothing to sell. But my wife said: 'No! You cannot put a sign in the window. For over 30 years your friends come to you for their blankets. A sign is too unfeeling. You go to Chicago, you be there when your friends come, you explain in person. You owe your friends at least that.' So here I am,"

About then he got *very* excited and said, "But wait, wait, where did you say you are from?" (I hadn't said.)

"Traverse City, Michigan."

"Oh my! Oh my! You are in luck! With this, he pulled a large bundle of telegrams from his coat pocket (he had a telegram for every person he talked to, no matter where they were from) and rifled through them, saying, "Oh my! Oh my! Oh! Oh! Oh! Yes, yes, here it is." Then he whipped out a telegram from a city 50 miles from Traverse City.

Really excited now, he said, "A dealer in Cadillac, Michigan, ordered 250 of my best-selling blankets, a blanket that is selling so well I cannot even take on new dealers. This company was foreclosed on and my blankets are in a bonded warehouse in Cadillac. I tell you what, because I want to help you and because you are such a trusted friend (I had just met him for the first time in my life) and valued customer (I had never bought from him or his company), I'm going to let you have those blankets. The freight is already paid to Cadillac. I will ship them on to Traverse City at no cost and even pay the warehouse fee in Cadillac. Then to make it an even better deal, I am going to give you 25% off on the hottest-selling blanket in the world."

Well, that's how a furniture company in Traverse City, Michigan, that didn't carry blankets got 250 blankets and, 33 years later, may still have them.

What a deal, what a deal!

The principle of this technique should be evident. Except for my story about the TV salesman, every one of these salespeople was using a phony story, but their promise of a better deal worked. The sad part of each story is that the technique could have been practiced with integrity and used to build rewarding careers yielding far more income.

Here's how this technique, when practiced with

integrity, can add thousands of dollars to your income every year:

All retail stores have items in every department that are reduced for one reason or another — they are discontinued, slow movers, scratched or dented, defective, and so on. Keeping up on this inventory can be a gold mine for you if you do it right. Always carry a note pad if you don't trust your memory. Certain items are needed constantly in most homes, so every time this sort of item is reduced, you have new ammunition.

Any time your company is about to have a sale and you can tell someone before the ad comes out, they have just gotten the first chance at a better deal.

Any time something new and different comes in and you can tell someone before anyone else knows about it, it is one of the strongest motivators. It is human nature to want to be the first kid on the block with one.

No matter where you are, no matter what you are doing, no matter who you are talking to, this subject can be brought up and you will find an eager listener every time. Everybody wants to hear about a better deal, and this will work even better when you talk to people away from your store.

Selling Outside of the Store

Let's say you're standing around outside church after services, visiting with other folks you know only casually. Of course, everyone is trying to be clever and conversational. Bright and witty questions are being asked, such as: "How's tricks?," "What's happening?," and so on. Most people respond with "Not much, what's happening with you?" If you respond with something like this, your listener will be all ears: "You wouldn't know anyone who might need a reclining chair, would you?" They will always ask "Why?"

The reason they ask is because if the deal is good enough, they are the ones who are going to need a reclining chair. You answer, "Well, (name of your company), the company I work for has marked down the price of all its floor samples to about one-half and if I could use one I would buy it myself . . ."

Don't be surprised when you quickly become the center of conversation. Human nature again. Everyone wants to get in on a good deal. But here's where we separate the professionals from the losers. Here's where the money's made.

You describe the item, the quality, the value, the comparisons, the fabric, the benefits, you make the customer want it because it is a better deal than he could ever hope to find on his own. Then you offer to hold it for him until he can come in to see it. With that, you whip out a sold tag and put his name, address, and phone number on it. Then you ask him when he can make it into the store. Be specific. Pin him down. Write the time of the appointment on the sold tag, give the prospect your card, and continue to greet the next person or group of people who are anxious to hear about a better deal.

Everybody's Interested in a Deal

Not long ago I attended an artist's show in the lobby of a large bank. I wandered from one painting to the next, visiting with people I knew and didn't know. One of the guards standing to the side of the hors d'oeuvres table asked: "Mr. Lawhon, my wife and I are thinking about getting a water bed. Do you have any good buys right now?"

If the TV camera had been on, it would have looked like one of those E. F. Hutton commercials. You could see everyone within hearing distance lean over to hear my answer, and by the time I had answered two or three questions, there was a crowd gathering. You would have thought that I had called a press conference. There were doctors, lawyers, bankers, teachers, guards — people of every walk of life instantly alerted to the possibility of getting in on the inside track. Without exception, they all wanted to hear about a better deal.

Here comes an even more surprising fact. The item or product is not the most important consideration. The *deal* is the most important part. If the deal is good enough, almost anyone will buy on the spot.

To increase the power of this technique, pick out an item that many people might be interested in and that you can make a better deal on. They will be all ears.

And therein lies the secret of this sales technique.

Remember, the only reason salespeople are needed is to provide a service. It is their job to provide the information necessary for the customer to make the best buying decision.

Second, remember the customer does not trust salespeople when he is on their own turf. As you have seen, when a customer goes into a retail store to try to fill his need, he has admitted the need and knows the chances are he will be assaulted, bumped, harassed, and basically annoyed by an incompetent salesperson who is probably less able to help him than he is to help himself. Yet this person is at the peak of his buying priority.

Now, let's look at these same people on their own turf, protected by familiar surroundings and people they trust. They're entirely different. How many times have you heard it said, "He is really a very nice person once you get to know him"? What they are really saying is that, taken away from one environment and placed in another, a person acts and reacts differently.

When people meet on a social level, they are wide open to a better deal. The E. F. Hutton commercials are always set in personal situations where confidential information is being exchanged.

THE CELLAR CLUB

When I lived in California, I was invited to become a member of an old and exclusive club that was limited to 132 members, each of whom had been invited to join because he met two criteria. He had to be at the very top of his profession, and there could be no other members with the same profession.

(Of course, there were several famous doctors, but each was in a different specialty. The same was true of attorneys. There were three, but one was a criminal lawyer, one a tax specialist, and one had a corporate practice. Other than that, the members ranged from a world-famous big game hunter to a world-famous custom car builder, from one of America's all-time great entertainers to men of stature in all businesses. We even had an astronaut.)

The club's sole purpose was a two-hour monthly gathering at which the only business discussed was business.

Everyone was free to ask and everyone was expected to give any information that might benefit the asking party. It was an honor to be invited to belong for two reasons: recognition by other men of achievement — a real highlight in any man's career — plus access to better deals. Even the most successful people in the world are interested in hearing about a better deal.

What's the difference between the robemaker in Cairo, the blanket salesman in Chicago, the clothier on State Street, the "grieving father" in Mexico, and all the others of their ilk, and the solid, respected business people who are successful in their own professions?

Honesty.

The world is full of phony good deals. Luckily, most of them are presented so crudely that most people spot their flaws right away.

THE BETTER DEAL AND ADVERTISING

The American advertising media are full of ads that promote out-and-out phony deals. Which makes the job of selling through advertising very difficult. Anyone who has a genuine better deal to offer finds the public so prejudiced against phony ad offers that they lump everything together and say it's all phony, or at least partially phony.

How do you feel about advertised items?

Let's say you need a new suit. The store advertises a special purchase of $300 suits on sale for $150. One-half price. You don't bother to check it out, because you have been there before and you know chances are pretty good that those suits aren't a good buy at $150 and would never have been sold at $300. Yet, a few men are gullible enough to respond.

P. T. Barnum said, "You can fool some of the people all of the time and all of the people some of the time." An international con artist recently convicted and sentenced to prison in a Tulsa, Oklahoma, Federal Court said "You can fool some of the people all of the time and all of the people some of the time. And that's good enough for me."

WHAT IS A BETTER DEAL?

If a good deal were easily defined, it wouldn't be so easy to falsify. There have never been and never will be any two deals exactly alike.

Simply stated, a good deal is one that offers a service or product whose benefits exceed the price paid.

Because the majority of benefits are emotional and emotions are personal, with no two persons being identical, it stands to reason that no two people can derive the same degree of benefit from any transaction, wouldn't you agree?

So here's the scene.

Everybody is tuned in all the time to the slightest whisper of a better deal.

Yes, the E. F. Hutton TV commercial has hit it right on the nose. When people believe they are going to hear about a better deal, *they listen!*

Anytime they listen it is because they are interested in the product. And anytime they are interested in a product it is because they either need it or think they need it or know someone else who does. Telling a friend about a better deal is sometimes even more exciting than finding one for yourself. ◄

Think about that last statement.

The most sought-after benefit in life is approval. When we tell someone important to us about a better deal, he rewards us with his thanks and approval, doesn't he? Sometimes, that's almost as good as buying the product yourself, because if it is a high priority need for him and a low priority need for you, it makes the deal for him even more fantastic and more exciting. And you get to bask in that excitement.

THE PROFESSIONAL IN THE PROFESSION

You have chosen retail selling for your profession. That's the way you are going to make your living. You are going to become a walking gold mine of information about better deals on your product.

Let's accept the fact that you have taken the challenge of your profession.

> YOU know your inventory.
> YOU know what your product is and what it does.
> YOU know your company's policies.

YOU know every detail of your company's financing.
YOU know your competition's product, which has
made you an authority on the best deals.
YOU know every item which your company is
willing to sell at a loss or reduced price.

Yes, you have made yourself a walking encyclopedia of better deals. You know of new and exciting things just arriving or on their way in, because some of the best deals involve being the first kid on the block to own something. In fact, within your store you are a self-contained business, but you still have to overcome the customer's distrust. As a professional, you have practiced your approach until it works almost without fail.

That's how you make your living.

By now, a small nagging thought may be creeping into your brain. An even bigger reservoir — yes, a veritable bottomless reservoir of customers, may be right there in front of you all the time. Are you getting the message? Is the real potential of this sales secret starting to become apparent to you?

Right in front of you every day are people who are anxious to hear about a better deal. There is not a soul you come in contact with who isn't anxious to hear of all those better deals you have bottled up inside of you.

Most of the time, they will even prod you for some of that valuable information with questions such as: "You don't have any good deals right now, do you?" or "When are you going to have a sale?"

Because I am well known in Tulsa and other cities, I rarely use any service or buy any product without the person who waits on me asking for inside information on a good deal on my product.

My experience goes like this almost every time:

Ticket-taker at airport: "Oh, you're John F. Lawhon, the furniture man. We bought our living room furniture at your store and just love it. When are you going to have a sale on reclining chairs?"

In the doctor's office while being examined: "When are you going to have your Posturpedic bedding on sale?"

In the grocery check-out line: "Oh, Mr. Lawhon, it's good to meet you. Do you have any good buys on TV sets?"

In restaurants my meal is often interrupted by patrons who recognize me and come over to introduce themselves. Seldom do they leave before they have asked if I am going to be having a sale soon on some particular item.

These examples reinforce the fact that all people, at all times, want to hear from an inside source about a better deal. Even if the deal has a very low priority level in the person's mind at the time, if the benefits promised far exceed the price asked, and urgency is added, the sale becomes a reality.

URGENCY

Urgency can be the greatest closing tool there is when it's used honestly. To understand this, reread the chapter about closing the sale.

By now, you're probably thinking "Sure — people ask you about better deals because you are the owner of the company and have been in your TV commercials." On the contrary, I have experienced this psychological phenomenon not only as owner, but also as general manager, factory worker, and salesman.

In the New Testament, there is a passage that says "A prophet is without honor save in his own country." Loosely translated, as owner, I am still less to be trusted as a source for a better deal for furniture than a second or less-interested party.

The other day, I took a business acquaintance to lunch. I picked him up in my new Mercedes 500 sedan which I am very proud of. As we started off, he said: "Wow! This is a great automobile. I didn't know you could get a '500' in the U.S."

I said, "You can't through regular channels, but I wanted the European model with the big engine, ABS brakes, and other features not available at that time on the American version. So I called all over the country getting quotes only to discover a guy right here in Tulsa, someone you know really well, who has about a dozen of them on hand right now."

He said, "Who is that?" I gave him the man's name. He said, "Sure, I know him, I handle all of his insurance. I'll just call him."

"You might do better if you call the salesman," I replied. "Negotiate only with him and you'll get the best price he's allowed to give."

Within two hours after lunch my friend had his new car.

What the Salesman Forgot

A little aside to this deal: my acquaintance advised the salesman that I had sent him over and that if he could have a car at the price I had paid for mine, he was ready to buy. A month later, I took my car in for a checkup. The car salesman had not yet even called me to thank me for a $50,000 sale. When I asked him if the sale to my business associate had gone well, he mumbled yes.

You can bet that should the occasion again arise to recommend him, I'll be most hesitant, because I — like every other human on this earth, the great and the small, the rich and the poor — love to get approval, and a phone call to thank me for sending him a customer would have been all it took to keep me working for him. Over a period of years, who knows how many thousands of dollars in commissions he could have reaped by writing orders on $50,000 cars which I had sold for him at no cost in time or money except a moment or two on the phone to express his thanks, thus permitting me the luxury of basking in his approval.

Remember this story any time you forget that follow-ups can add thousands of dollars to your income.

My Mercedes-hunting friend was a man to whom the five or six thousand dollars he saved on the new car was a pittance. Yet, he could not be moved to buy until he thought he was getting a better deal.

Any time you get to thinking that anyone you meet, a factory worker, professional, or even the President of the United States, is not interested in hearing about your better deal, think again. That desire is universal, as much a part of all human beings as their heart, lungs, brain and blood.

Watch out now. Here comes the double whammy. Which came first? The hearing about the better deal or the telling about it? It is just as hard to determine which the human animal (who loves a better deal) would rather do — *hear about a better deal, or . . . tell about a better deal.*

Sometimes, I think the driving force that makes us all want to hear so desperately about a better deal, that moves our buying priority all the way to the top of our list when we think we can get one, that causes us to take immediate buying action, really stems from the deep-seated need we all have to *tell* about the better deals.

Then we can bask in the envy, praise and imagined approval of everyone we come in contact with.

41

BOOSTING YOUR INCOME WITH A BETTER DEAL

To be sure you fully understand them, you may have to go back and reread entire portions of this section. Learning about the better deal can be the most important single bonus technique of your career. Properly practiced, it can not only add to your present income, it can literally *multiply* your income *many times over.*

> **I don't care how high your sales earning is right now, if you don't fully understand the psychology of the better deal and are not taking full advantage of it, you are living way below your potential income level.**

Let me show you how this works in practice.

Suppose you are a salesman working eight hours a day, five days a week and you are busy waiting on and selling customers during every one of those hours. Therefore, it is impossible for you to multiply your sales many times over. After all, there is only one of you and you are operating at your peak during every working hour and you are head and shoulders above any other salesperson competing with you. You have the highest sales volume and you have the highest income and there is no doubt you are the best.

Think again!

Let's examine the salesman who sold me the Mercedes. On a scale of one to ten, considering all the car salespeople I have known, I'd rate him as a nine. He was very good. He knew his product and he knew his inventory. He demonstrated and showed me every feature the car offered. He translated every feature into several benefits. He knew his warranties and company policies. At no time did he have to ask anyone else for any assistance. I was paying cash, so he did not have to know anything about finance. While we were finalizing the contracts, the phone rang.

He excused himself while he wrote down the approval information from the money covering a car he had set up on a lease plan. I heard the name of the lessor and knew him well. I asked why Dick would be leasing a car. He could pay cash for a fleet of them. The salesman said, "Yes, but in Dick's case, there were considerable tax advantages for him in leasing." So he had found the most favorable source for the lease. And this conversation caused me to believe that he also really knew his financing.

When I called the first time, the salesman was very busy and in order to see him I made an appointment for late that afternoon. I already knew the car, the prices, and the color I wanted, so it would seem all he had to do was give me the better deal and send me on my way.

Not quite.

By the time the car had been demonstrated and each of its features explained, from how to operate the jack to the safety key, over an hour of that salesperson's time had been consumed. The customer I sent over had been so totally pre-sold because I had pointed out and demonstrated every one of the features to him that the second sale required less than a fourth the time of my sale. Furthermore, the second buyer probably will have many more occasions to brag about his "better deal" than I will, and he can be expected over the years to keep a flow of pre-sold buyers calling that salesperson on a fairly regular basis.

It doesn't take much of a brain to see that if that salesperson had started with even one or two receivers of a better deal (such as me or my associate) and each were kept active with that recognition and approval that we all thrive on, his life would become one of clipping coupons.

Of course, he would still have to keep up-to-date on his product, what it was and how it worked, financing, company policies, and warranties, but with four times the money rolling in, he could probably convince the owner to furnish him an assistant to handle the detail work, leaving him time to increase his income even more, or to just relax and enjoy the fruits of his success.

Sounds alarmingly simple, doesn't it? Well, let me assure you, it is even simpler than it sounds, because success in selling is governed by a simple law of nature.

Obviously, none of these exciting things is going to happen unless you have built a solid base. Your confidence must be well-grounded and you must be anxious to exercise your professional skills. This will be the case if you are following all of the directions given up until now in this book — far and beyond the call of duty.

THE (FOOL'S) GOLD RUSH — POOR PREPARATION

In 1849, gold was discovered in California. It caused one of the greatest mass-migrations in the history of our nation. Men by the thousands (and a few women) took any means at hand to reach California. Families were abandoned, farms deserted, children suddenly made fatherless. Men gave up everything just to get there.

They sold all their earthly possessions for whatever money they would bring. By wagon, mule, ox, horse, ship or foot the trip was made. Hundreds died in the effort, and when they arrived, only a very few ever discovered enough gold even to keep themselves fed.

They went to California without knowledge, experience, or equipment. Their failure was guaranteed. Even the few who did find gold passed over far more than they recovered because of the primitive way the gold was mined. When the rush was over and the smoke had cleared away, those who one way or another had gathered together the knowledge, the experience and the equipment and put it all into operation were the only ones left and they, the very few, wound up with all the claims and all the mines.

So, back to you — this walking gold mine you have made of yourself. It is all of little or no use if you can't get the ore out, smelted into pure gold, transferred to your bank and available to use as you desire. The homes will never be bought, the cars never owned, the university educations never gained, the sweet smell of success never enjoyed, and the comforting reward of a financially secure future never known — unless you do this.

If you have reviewed everything up to here and have sure confidence in your ability to make yourself into a walking gold mine, and you still have that ever-present requirement needed to succeed — desire — then let's learn how to mine that gold without letting even the tiniest flake escape.

USING THE BETTER DEAL TO YOUR ADVANTAGE: THE CRITICAL SECOND STEP

Miraculously, you have passed from infancy into full-grown adulthood as a salesperson in almost the twinkling of an eye. You are already enjoying added income, satisfaction and recognition. The fruits of your success are very sweet and more than likely have whetted your desire for even greater success. Your knowledge of inventory, product, financing, warranties, and your company's policies is complete and up-to-date. Your company is bursting at the seams with better deals and you are aware of new ones coming on the market almost hourly. You are ready to learn the secret of getting the gold out.

The first step is easy. It is natural that you will tell anyone who will listen about your better deals, even without being told to. Human nature, remember? Just as natural and as much a part of you as your lungs, heart, brain and blood.

But if you don't have a good plan for turning your listener's excitement into a sale and collecting the commission, all your labors up to now will be in vain.

So here is the absolutely critical step two: Tell about your better deal *with closing a sale as your only objective.* Let's see how that might work.

THE LUNCH HOUR SALE

Here you are, eating lunch in one of your regular haunts. The owner comes over and asks, "How's your meal?" You say something like: "Delicious — and the extra vegetables are helping me with my diet." The owner then asks, "By the way, when are you folks going to have another sale on your bedding?" You ask, "What do you need?" "Oh, the wife and I have been talking about a king-size, but we'd have to have a new bed and bedding to go with it."

You look around to see that no one else is listening, lower your voice, lean closer, and tell him about one of your better deals.

"I was going through our shop this morning and I saw a brand new Posturpedic queen-size sleep set, ready to go into the outlet department. The warehouseman had backed the order picker against the side and gotten grease on it. The shop removed the grease, but it still left a very light stain that would not come out. Other than that, the set is perfect and still carries the Sealy 15-year warranty. We even have expando-rails to fit your present bed slots that will let you put that queen size right onto your present bed. Because the queen size is only six inches wider and six inches longer than your double bed, if you just buy new fitted sheets for the mattress, your full-size top sheets and blankets should be just fine.

"More important than that, there isn't any doubt today that the Sealy Posturpedic has the best reputation in the industry. It got that reputation for building a quality sleep set that gave a night's sleep as good as or better than any other set you can buy. After all, that's what you are really after — a good night's sleep, wouldn't you agree?

"Well, I have to run, because my lunch hour is almost over. Let me recommend this before I go. That set sells for $569 at all quality Sealy dealers in our city. It's the Imperial Model and you can call any department store to verify the price.

"This one is reduced to $399 and I am sure that the first bedding customer who sees it will grab it because that's what we charge for our lowest-price set. Why don't I just hurry back and put a sold tag on it until you can come in to see it?"

He mumbles a little but agrees. With that, you whip out a sold tag and proceed to fill it out as you ask what would be the best time for him and his wife to drop by, this afternoon or some time this evening? If he says this evening, you say, "Great! Listen, I usually finish dinner around 6:30 and I could be waiting when you arrive or would later in the evening be better?"

If at any point he hesitates on tying himself down, just hang loose. Don't give up until you have a reasonably firm commitment from him. Of course, you leave him with your card tucked firmly into his wallet.

If you plan it right and do a good job when he comes in, which we will cover later in this chapter, you can afford to eat lunch in the very finest restaurants, make enough to pay for lunch, and even cover the lease payments on that new Cadillac so you can arrive first class.

Remember now, we have agreed that you were already enjoying a very successful career and above-average income before you ventured out to mine gold from the better deal. So what you make at lunch becomes the bonus.

Think about that — I bet that you have never had a lunch as exciting and rewarding as the one I have just described.

Baloney, you say. That's only one lunch and one owner. You can't tell me this will work every time or that the same thing will happen every time I have lunch in a different restaurant.

Uh oh! You have cheated — you went ahead and passed the stop bar before you understood the principle of the better deal.

If you agreed with the preceding baloney reaction, quit lying to yourself and go back over the concept section until you understand it and know that you understand it.

If you disagreed with the baloney remark, you have passed the first test and you're well on your way.

Of course, the restaurant example has only one in a thousand chances of ever happening even close to the way I described it, but in principle it can and should happen at least once every lunch hour to the master of the better deal.

You are bursting with better deals, you are in a public place for lunch, you have an opportunity to enter into conversations with many different people, any one of whom is eager for and avidly seeking a better deal.

So start the ball rolling. Join any conversation — after all, those conversations are almost always just pleasantries. You and you alone have entered that conversation prepared to tell about a better deal. Only you have the genuine article.

Remember, when E. F. Hutton talks, everybody listens. That may be considered advertising license, but I can assure you that when the bearer of the better deal talks and it's the genuine thing, everybody will listen. Present the better deal, along with a plan to close the sale. Then stop and listen and you will hear the customer's buying priority gears shift.

THE BETTER DEAL IS GENUINE

Before I get further into buying priorities, let me explain a genuine better deal. In order for the Posturpedic sleep set mentioned earlier to have been a better deal, every word of what I said had to be true — *every word!*

> It's not a better deal if it requires even one little bitty lie to substantiate it.

If we have that straight, let's look at how buying priorities are changed by a genuine better deal.

In 1963, I was on the rostrum as an advertiser at a state convention of American Women in Radio and Television. Preceding me was an internationally known psychologist who was considered an authority on buyer motivation through electronic media.

The thrust of his speech was that we ("we" being the advertisers) try to reach people with our product at the wrong times. For example, he said, when I am home sitting in my easy chair, watching TV while my wife is in the kitchen preparing dinner, I am getting hungrier by the minute as the rich, savory aromas of her cooking float into where I am sitting. Then, he said, is not the time to talk to me about anything except something to eat. The closer it gets to dinner time, the hungrier I get and the less chance you have of selling me anything but food.

He sat down to a burst of thunderous applause. I was announced next and it was my job to explain my position as the advertiser. As I write this, what happened 21 years ago is still vividly clear in my memory.

This was my opening statement:

"Sir, if I accept what you say, I believe I might as well go into some other business. I have to believe that no matter how hungry you are or how busy your wife is, what I must do is reach through your mind with a *good enough deal* to make a buyer out of you."

He interrupted me and said, "Young man, you would be wasting your time."

"Doctor, I can give you an example of an offer that could make your wife leave the dinner to burn while she hung on my every word, slowing down only long enough to grab you, her purse, and turn the stove off, before she rushed you out the door and forced you to speed to my store. Upon arrival, she'd leap from the car, race to get in line, and stand there in line all night long or until the last item I had to offer was gone."

The doctor sat speechless and the audience was stunned by my audacity. Remember, I was speaking to women and this was 1963.

"Doctor, let's just suppose that as you are watching the news, the announcer says: 'We want to interrupt our newscast to take you live to the parking lot of Evans Home Furnishings, where a train wreck occurred about two hours ago. This will break the hearts of any women who are watching.' With that, they switch to a live camera.

'As many of you know,' the announcer continues, 'the Rock Island tracks from Chicago to Dallas cross Western Avenue right at Evans' property line bordering the parking lot.' The camera shows two or three freight cars rolled over on their sides and one is split wide open.

"The camera zooms in on one and the announcer, who is rifling through its spilled contents, says: 'This has to be one of the most sickening sights many of you women watching will ever see. This 40-foot freight car was packed solid with the entire Christmas stock of Neiman-Marcus' fur coats. Look at them scattered here. Minks, sable, fox, lynx, and dozens so rare I can't even identify them.

'These coats would all have to sell for over $1,000 and many of them would go for over $10,000. Why, there must be two or three thousand of them.

'Fortunately, no one was injured in the wreck. The railroad people have been here almost since it happened, and they assure me it will all be cleared up shortly.' Doctor, if your wife could hear the announcer from the kitchen, the chances are several thousand to one that she stepped into the den to watch.

"Now, let's suppose that an hour or two earlier, the railroad insurance adjuster had arrived and, of course, I would have been out watching the proceedings on my parking lot, even though the police had cordoned off the entire area. I made the salvage agents a cash offer on the spot for the coats, as is, and they took it. I already own a one-minute spot late in the newscast you are watching. I jump in my car and race to the TV station just in time to go on live for one minute.

"Slightly out of breath, I say, 'Ladies, listen quick. You just saw the news bulletin about the train wreck that happened at our store. You saw the fur coats bound for Neiman-Marcus spewed all over our parking lot. They retail for $1,000 to $10,000. I made an offer to the salvage agents for them and bought them. There are over 2,000 of them. Get in your car, rush to our store, get in line, because we are going to start selling them first come, first served. The person next in line each time a coat is pulled out of the freight car will get that coat, whatever kind, size or price it is and it will be strictly one to a customer. But now, hear this. They will be $50 each until the last one is gone!

"Doctor," I said, "your wife might not even slow down to turn off the stove as she heads for my store." (But no one heard me, I was getting a standing ovation.)

Then I went on to explain that in spite of people's primary needs, if I hoped to be successful, I had to overcome those buying priorities. Every time I did a TV commercial, I tried to make it as exciting and as urgent as my fantasy account of that train wreck.

Great sales success comes only to those who *refuse* to concede
▶ competitors' claims for a higher buyer priority for their product or service, by continually searching out and making people aware of a better deal.

THE BETTER DEAL REORDERS PRIORITIES

You've heard my made-up story of how a buying priority might be changed. Let me tell you a true story of how 18 buying priorities were changed radically all at once.

In 1966 or thereabouts, the headlines were full of the Billie Sol Estes scandal. The wire services carried a picture of a pair of men's alligator shoes that Billie Sol had bought at Neiman-Marcus for $148 and given to some crooked politician. Shortly before the release of the picture, Neiman's had a fire. Although only a small part of their inventory was damaged, they announced that the entire inventory would be sold to liquidators outside of their trade area. None of these liquidators would be allowed to make any public announcements that in any way hinted at or included the Neiman-Marcus name.

The day the picture of the $148 shoes appeared in the Oklahoma City paper, there was a large group of men who had gathered around my office and we were preparing to go out to lunch together. The paper was on my desk and those $148 shoes had became the topic of conversation when the side door of the building swung open and a factory rep came rushing in, all out of breath. Between gasps, he blurted, "Fellas, I just came from a little salvage store in a town 40 miles from here and guess what? I saw the entire Neiman-Marcus men's shoe stock from the fire including all of their alligators and he is selling them for $30 a pair!"

Before he had finished and before you could count to ten, 18 grown men were burning rubber off the tires of three Cadillacs, breaking all the speed laws on their way to a store 40 miles away.

Before that salvage dealer knew what had hit him, we'd cleaned him out. (I got six pairs of alligator shoes, a pair of alligator boots, seven pairs of house shoes, and a pair of patent leather tuxedo shoes. The boots, house shoes and tux shoes I have to this day.)

I remember the shoes, but I can't tell you whether we ever ate lunch or not. (And, note too, that factory rep drove at a high rate of speed over 40 miles just to be able to tell us about a better deal!)

Now that, my friends, is a true story I recently reconfirmed with two of the participants. I doubt there is a man alive who was present who would not have had his buying priorities changed instantly just like ours were. Even his thoughts, like ours of the lunch we were about to enjoy, would have been completely washed away in the rush to our cars.

That was definitely a better deal. By the way, the full alligator boots I bought that day cost me $50. What a deal!

These two stories should help you understand how the priorities are reordered when someone hears about a better deal and just how wild the response can be.

These better deals excited the public for three reasons:
1. They were all sensational deals.
2. They were absolutely true.
3. The public believed them.

The beauty of the better deal is that jumping at it is the natural thing to do.

When you tell someone else about that good deal you got, you're working for someone else. You might've even made the sale for them, just as I did with the $50,000 Mercedes. I never collected one dime in commissions.

But now you are a professional salesperson; you work on commis- ◀
sion. If you are going to tell about better deals (and you are) at least
tell about your own company's better deals and follow through on ◀
each one. Get the sale. Collect the commission. It's the easiest, highest paying work there is.
What a deal! What a deal!

42

Service Beyond the Call of Duty

THE MARK OF GREATNESS

I have made thousands of sales even when my price was the not the lowest, because my customer owed me too much not to buy from me. Let me explain that "debt."

I have always gone out of my way to be of service to my customers. That personal service creates a *value.*

"Mrs. Jones, I have a lamp I think would be perfect for you. Sit right there. I'll be right back." Off I go at a fast trot, quickly returning with the lamp. I plug it in and turn it on. A little out of breath I ask, "How does that look?" I may gather a dozen lamps before I make the sale, but I always make it because with every lamp I bring back, Mrs. Jones owes me a little more. (When you are finished, be sure to put everything back in place immediately.)

I'd find a sofa my customer liked only to have her ask what chair would go with it. I never asked her to follow me. I took the sofa cushion and found the chair that goes with it best and back I'd come carrying the chair. Always a little out of breath and somewhat strained, I'd lower the chair into place next to the sofa, saying, "You really can't tell how a chair will look with a sofa unless you see them side-by-side." After a couple of chairs, the customer was too embarrassed to go somewhere else to buy. Anytime I had the opportunity to do anything for my customer, I took it. I didn't walk either, I ran, coming back always a little out of breath.

▶ Early on, I learned that the best salesperson renders service cheerfully. Whenever my customer gave me a chance to render a service, I rushed to take advantage of it. When they didn't, I tried to create opportunities to render a service.

"Mrs. Jones, let me turn this chair over so that you can see underneath it," I'd say, grunting a little and straining ever so slightly as I turned it over. As I straightened up, I was just a little out of breath.

"Mrs. Jones, what color is your carpet?" Then off to the carpet department to get all the samples that I thought would resemble the color she had described. Spreading the carpet samples out in front of her, I took a deep breath as if to regain the breath I had lost in my rush.

Here's a secret that can make you seem like a super salesperson while you master the profession of selling. Kill your customers with enthusiastic kindness!

This isn't new. I was taught it first by some of the true masters of retail selling: Jewish merchants along lower State Street in Chicago.

One of my favorites always took on a look of sheer panic as he flicked his hand across a customer's shoulder, knocking an imaginary spider to the floor and quickly stepping on it, then grinding it underfoot he shouted, "Mein Gott! A spider on your shoulder!"

He had just rendered me the service of saving my life from a deadly spider that existed only in his mind. Before I had recovered from my peril he was brushing lint from my collar and untucking the flap on my coat pocket.

By then, the value of his services was really piling up. Then he said, "You look so good in that suit. I bet you are a perfect 38 long." (In the early '50s, I was.) "I would be proud to have anyone who wears a suit as well as you do wearing one of my suits."

Shortly after my wife and I were married in 1968, she wondered aloud why I always waited until business took me to Chicago to buy my suits. Now she knows. There was a seller of suits there, who, I believe to this day, was proud that I wore his suits and besides, on at least six occasions, he saved my life from deadly spiders.

His desire to be of service was genuine and if he had to create a few spiders and a little lint to keep in practice, so be it. I always knew deep inside, had that been a real spider on my shoulder and had it been deadly, he'd still have risked his life to knock it off. So, I never held it against him if he wanted to keep in practice when it came to being of service to me.

That man demanded the very best of his tailors, the very best of his staff and, yes, if I wanted to wear my new suit out of his shop, he always saw to it that the tailoring was done at once to my satisfaction.

The attitude that "it's not my job" has never been part of the professional salesperson's personality. Instead, he sees the opportunity to serve as another chance to sell, just an extension of his profession. When his customer buys a lamp and wants to take it with her, he doesn't just offer to carry it to her car. A professional would rather fight than to give up that opportunity to further serve. He *insists* on carrying the lamp to her car.

When a professional sees a crooked picture on the wall, he even excuses himself for a moment to straighten it at once. That respect for his product is quickly noted by his customer.

These acts of courtesy and service are the visible signs of the professional. That extra effort makes you feel better as you greet your next customer, knowing you are going to sell again. Added personal service certainly creates added value for your product or service.

How many times have you gone to a restaurant where the service was so good you left a larger tip than usual or (as is more often the case) was so bad you left no tip?

In one case, added service created added value. In the other, less than normal service took away value, so you not only left no tip, but probably resented having to pay for the food.

> **Added services make you customers for life.**
>
> **Receiving less service than they are entitled to will keep customers from coming back.**
>
> **Every professional gives the added service that creates customers for life.**

When one salesperson told me he sent thank-you cards only to customers who made big purchases, I asked him who he thought would appreciate his thank-you card the most, the person who just spent $10,000 or, the one who had only spent $50? The $10,000 customer expected it; to the $50 customer it would have been a pleasant surprise. More important, who do you think will be making a large purchase next? The customer who just made one or the customer who didn't?

Don't quibble. Send every person you wait on a thank-you card, *especially* those who don't buy or those who make only small purchases. A thank-you card is a small extra service, just like a sincere compliment. When you send a card to the person who bought $10,000 worth of furniture, it is expected. For the customer whom you made every effort to help but who did not buy, it is a giant extra service that leaves that customer in your debt and a red-hot prospect to a professional.

Courtesy costs nothing is an old adage. Not only doesn't it cost, it ◀ pays, and it pays big. Those services you perform for your customer that are above and beyond the call of duty are going to pay off in plus-sales and commissions for years.

Service beyond the call of duty makes customers *yours* for life.

43

GETTING YOUR HOUSE
IN ORDER

How you dress, your personal hygiene and habits, even your voice and hair can cost you sales. What you do, what you wear, what you say, and how you groom yourself must be acceptable to your customer.

Take musk-based cologne. It has a residual effect that increases in potency each time you use it. Each time you wear it, you must add a little more in order for you to smell it yourself. As a result, you wear more and more each time. Add that to the scent already locked in your clothes and hair and soon it becomes too much.

Your customers who don't use musk colognes or perfumes are repelled by the odor and some may even be allergic to it. It may not cost you a sale every time, but it will eventually. So why begin with a negative? Mild scents used sparingly are the answer. This act of courtesy applies to salesmen as well as women.

No one should have to be told about body odor, bad breath, yellow teeth, dirty eyeglasses, unpressed or soiled clothing. These can all be very offensive and extremely distracting for your customer. A customer simply cannot buy from you if you have bad breath or body odor. Personal hygiene neglected (for *one* day) will cost you sales.

How you wear your hair is important. Today, the general public is much more tolerant of hair styles than ten years ago, but there are still some very good rules to follow if you would rather not lose any sales. If your hair style is not acceptable to the majority of the customers you are going to be waiting on, change it. Remember, I am assuming you will be selling at the mass-market level, and as a rule of thumb that means conservative customers. Anything extreme will offend them.

The revelation, "The Pupil of the Eye," stated that most of the time when you have a negative reaction to the customer, communication breaks down. It happens just as fast when the customer has a negative reaction to you.

Most men and women have a negative reaction to any man who wears his shirt unbuttoned two or more buttons and who wears a necklace. That appearance might be acceptable in some areas of the country but, even there he could still be offensive to a few. No professional can afford wasted time or the possibility of a lost sale.

Beards and moustaches are another area of concern. Thomas E. Dewey ran against Franklin D. Roosevelt for the office of President of the United States in 1944. One poll result showed that Dewey's moustache cost him the presidency.

I have done more than 50,000 different television commercials. I had never worn a moustache. But in 1980, I went elk hunting and let my beard grow. When I got back home, I shaved off everything but my moustache, then video-taped one session of TV commercials wearing my moustache. I got dozens and dozens of letters objecting to it.

I sported that moustache during that one session four years ago in commercials that ran for only one week on TV. To this day, people refer (always negatively) to the time I wore the moustache. Not a single person (including my own mother) ever told me they liked it. Not one letter told me how great it looked. Early on in the field of television advertising, I learned that if you received a single letter objecting to something you did or said on a commercial, there were thousands of viewers who were offended to some extent, no matter how minor.

You'll pay a very dear price in time and sales lost if you insist on wearing a beard, no matter how becoming it is. Your biggest hurdle in selling is gaining customers' confidence. As it happens, there are a lot of retail buyers out there who instinctively distrust men with moustaches and, to a far greater degree, men with beards.

The better you dress, the better you feel. The better you feel, the more you are going to sell. An investment in a good quality, simply tailored business wardrobe will pay for itself many times over.

Women who overdress for selling often make their customers uncomfortable. A low-cut dress with cleavage showing is a perfect example. You are going to make more sales faster if your clothes show good taste, are comfortable and are not distracting. Anything more or less will slow down your productivity.

Men can dress "too sharp," too. This doesn't necessarily offend a woman, but it will create an atmosphere of distrust. Men are actually offended more often by the over-dressed dandy.

Smoking and drinking are habits that are killers of sales. Alcohol on your breath means you are *drunk* to most of the people you will serve. Your service manager knows how violent some customers can become when a problem arises after a sale during which they smelled alcohol on the salesperson's breath. And those were customers who bought anyway. For every one of those, there were probably dozens of customers who smelled alcohol and didn't buy.

There's nothing worse than a reformed smoker and the world is full of them. I am one. Reformed smokers, for the most part, resent anyone around them smoking. Many people resent your smoking even though they smoke, because Americans are being taught that smoking is bad. They are not proud of it. They have built a resentment toward those who smoke. The professional never smokes in the presence of a customer, because it just doesn't pay.

Go on smoking, if you must. If full consideration is given to other people and your product, it won't affect the success of your career (unless it shortens it).

There is one hard and fast rule that should be a law in all furniture and clothing stores. No pipes or cigars allowed! Smoke from pipes and cigars will permeate fabrics and stay there. Many people are offended by cigar smoke and the clothes of cigar smokers reek of the odor. If you smoke cigars, you are probably not aware of the odor, just as the woman who wears ten times too much perfume and can't smell it on herself. Smoking cigars and pipes in a furniture store or clothing store costs sales for you and your employer in many ways.

Experts were inclined to agree that Walter Mondale lost his presidential election due to his voice, which they described as whining with pleading qualities. Likewise, his running mate, Geraldine Ferraro, possessed an undesirably strident voice with a brittle timbre.

Their voices? But they can't help that! Yes, they can and they sought help late in the campaign and improved their delivery, but by then it was too late.

Audiotape your voice. Listen to it. Listen for irritating elements. The small cost in time and money for a good voice coach can make you a lot of money. Usually, voice flaws can be corrected easily, once detected, and probably in only a matter of days.

Summarizing, I may seem picky and you may say that these things aren't all that important. No, they are *critically* important. If you are saying to yourself right now, "If they don't want to buy from me because I wear a moustache then they can just go to H---!" you lose. You lose with that attitude, which will cause your ultimate failure.

So, get your house in order. Your personal hygiene, dress and habits can have a negative effect on your career, or they can help you build your career. As with all the other teachings in this book, it is up to you.

44

GETTING THE JOB YOU WANT

T here is so much demand for professional salespeople all over the world that you should have no trouble getting a job. Getting the job that's best for you is another story.

Before you consider which job is best for you, you must determine which job you are going to do best.

Ask yourself, "Can I be loyal to that company?" You must think long and hard about your own integrity, for the first defect that emerges in all weak salespeople is disloyalty to the company for which they work.

As I have interviewed sales applicants over the years, I have learned that those who had nothing good to say about their former employers could be counted on to be disloyal employees. Disloyalty shows up most when employees bitch about company policies, benefits, products and services but there are multitudes of additional complaints.

Examine your own past record. Have I just described your attitude? Then you were disloyal to your employer. If, in fact, you have all those complaints about the company you work for, then quit. If you feel that your company has everything wrong with it and you don't quit (whether you bitch about it or not) you are being disloyal both to your employer and to yourself.

The first thing you owe any employer is loyalty, because it is his money that pays you for your labors. When you ask yourself what you can do for a company, ask first if you can be loyal. Be very sure you believe with all your heart that you can be proud to be working for the company and can remain loyal to it.

Once, when I was very young, I was offered a job as manager of a large and well-established company with an excellent reputation in the high end of the furniture business. I took it. I hated it. Oh, I loved the beautiful and expensive furniture, but I disliked the arrogance of the customers. They were never as excited about having an elegant new piece of furniture in their home as mass-market customers are. Since then, I have seen many salespeople fail because they didn't like the class of customers they served.

Sometimes, salespeople develop an arrogant, holier-than-thou attitude toward the customer that hinders communication and stops sales cold.

Review the revelation entitled "Empathy vs. Sympathy." If you don't have a good feeling about the class of customers attracted by your company, you stand little chance of success.

During my interviews, I questioned sales staffs of one company with two types of stores. One type carried popularly-priced furniture, the other only the highest-priced lines. Most of the salespeople I interviewed in the popularly-priced store expressed a desire to someday sell furniture in the high-priced store. I could easily see how it would be difficult, if not impossible, for them to adapt to the customers drawn to a high-end store.

The weak salespeople at the high-end store, more often than not, showed deep-seated resentment toward their more demanding high-end customers. So think long and hard about the people/customers you like before you begin to work for a company. The question arises again: What can you do for your company? Can you like, respect and be loyal to its customers?

Next, the company's image is important to your success. If you cannot say you are proud to be working for that company, you cannot be proud to sell their product and your failure is practically guaranteed. Those who can succeed when not proud of their product are hustlers and con artists.

Every authority on selling agrees that the first consideration in selling success is what the salesperson thinks of his product.

> Ask yourself again: How strongly can you feel about
> (1) your company, and (2) your customers? You must
> feel just as strongly that your customers will be
> better off exchanging their money for the enjoyment
> of the benefits of your product.

Often, when considering a company, a very important factor is overlooked. Does the more successful company offer the greater opportunity? Not necessarily! Often in a large company, competent management is already in place and sales staffs are effective. Therefore, your chances to excel are reduced.

On the other hand, those companies with weaker management and sales organizations offer a greater opportunity because their needs are greater. Should management be your goal, then the latter may be for you. Also, you may have observed how weak salespeople leave many customers alone to browse because they have no selling techniques. This means that a great sales potential is ripe for the picking.

> **Be sure that you know and understand a company's policies before you go to work for it. You can learn this by visiting with the salespeople who work for that company.**

Here comes my most important tip: To find out what a company can mean to you, you must ask the salespeople working there, both the best and the worst. When the question, What can you do for the company? is asked again, question yourself. Can you be conscientious enough to do a better job with more loyalty than those employees you visited with?

When you apply for a job, you should already know that you want to go to work for that company and be ready to tell them why. Don't be surprised if the owner or manager faints or has a heart attack when you not only give him all the reasons why you want to work for his company but back it up with all the things you believe you can do for his company. And don't be surprised when that owner/manager takes a personal interest in the development of your career.

Until a few years ago, companies were allowed to give aptitude and I.Q. tests to prospective employees. I have read and analyzed thousands of these tests and with a Detroit Clerical and an Otis I.Q. test, I can tell you every time whether an applicant can or cannot learn to sell at the retail level. I just can't tell you if he *will*.

Only He Can Determine Whether He Will!

Rarely is it a question of whether you can or can't sell, but whether you will or won't sell in any given place or situation.

Once you've decided who you want to work for and have read the chapter "Getting Your House in Order," then you must plan your strategy to get the sales job you want.

You simply sell yourself.

You have actually qualified the need of the company. You know who their best salesperson is. You know who is the worst, and why. You only need 90 days to prove yourself better than the worst and only a little longer to be one of the top producers for that company. Convince that company, then do it. It takes guts. It takes confidence in yourself, but when you have done your homework on the prospective company, the battle is nearly won.

Next, make a list of your selling points.

1. *You* have done thorough research on their company and have selected them.

2. You are burning with desire to sell their products, because you believe their customers will truly be better off when enjoying the benefits of those products.

3. You selected them after your research because you knew you could be loyal to them. You believe in their advertising approach. You believe in their merchandise. You believe in their company policies. Their customers are the kind of people you can relate to.

4. You have studied (not just read) this book and you believe that if you are given 90 days to learn everything you need to know while you develop techniques you are already working on, you will be one of their most productive salespeople.

5. You can be relied on. If it is your day to work, you will be there early. No meeting will be delayed because of you. No customer will have to wait. No door will not be opened because of you. Ever. Not one time.

6. You will always give that extra effort. It is a commitment you have made to yourself and you bring that commitment to the company you work for.

7. You work for nothing. You do not expect your company to pay you one dime until you earn it. You only earn it when you make a sale. (This is critical to your success. You expect to make a lot of money because you expect to sell a lot. If you don't, you have failed in your commitment to yourself and your company!)

8. They will never have to fire you. If you don't give them the results, the sales they have a right to expect, you will quit.

9. You don't give up if you are not hired the first time you try. After all, you have done your homework. You know this is the best company for you at this time. You are going to work for them and no one else. (You must develop this attitude and I assure you it will raise your confidence level to an all-time high.)

Can't you just sense the excitement you are going to radiate as you wait on that company's customers? If you have really committed yourself to sell this company on hiring you, it will probably be the easiest sale you will ever make.

One more time. Don't give up. Your chances of a successful selling career are multiplied many, many times if you make this sale. If they say NO, you ask "WHY?" and keep asking "why" to their answers. You are going to get that job with them because you are going to succeed in selling them and when you succeed, they will hire you. They will be the big winners. If you don't quit in your effort to get the job you want, you are not going to quit on those tough sales that mean the difference between the great and the near-great. And that is going to mean *a lot more net profit for your company*. Yes, you can. You will get that job and you will be a great one.

While writing this chapter, I was reminded of my first real job. February 12, 1944, I arrived home from helping my father at his job. He had left earlier and the other men on the job had brought me home.

There was a black funeral car in our driveway. My father's car had been hit by a train. He was dead. The funeral was two days later and by then, although I was in my early teens, I knew I must get a job and make my own way in the world. World War II was in full swing. I wasn't the only one who was afraid.

I decided that I wanted to work for B & M Rothchild's Company in downtown Oklahoma City for whatever reason a young boy decides those things. The day after my father's funeral, I got up early and went to the high school where I was in the tenth grade. I made arrangements to start on a special schedule that would allow me to leave school every day at 11:45. I applied for a work permit, being only 14 years old. I planned that I could be at Rothchild's by noon every weekday to go to work. I could also work all day on Saturday (and every night, if need be).

The next morning, I got out of bed early, dressed in my best clothes, and caught the trolley downtown. By 8:00 a.m., I had talked my way past the guard and was sitting on a wooden bench on the sixth floor of Rothchild's, just outside the office of Mr. Beasley, the personnel manager. I sat very straight, trying to look taller, with my hands folded in my lap as one executive after another, including Mr. Beasley, passed by on the way to their offices. As soon as Mr. Beasley's secretary arrived, I told her I wished to see Mr. Beasley because I needed a job and I wanted to work for B & M Rothchild's Company.

Shortly, she came back and told me that they didn't need anyone at that time and Mr. Beasley was very busy. I said, "That's OK, I will wait."

All during that day, a rather short man seemed to be coming and going out of the offices more than the others, passing me each time. When 4:00 p.m. came and I was still sitting on that wooden bench very straight with my hands folded in my lap, the rather short gentleman rushed by again but this time he stopped and asked me, "Young man, how long have you been sitting on that bench?"

"Since 7:40 this morning."

"Why?"

"I need a job. I want to work for this company. So, I am going to wait here until Mr. Beasley will see me." Whereupon, he reached down and grabbed my skinny wrist and jerked my 100-pound body to my feet. Without a word, he pulled me through two doors to an office. A man was sitting behind a large desk. The gentleman pushed me up in front of the desk and said, "Mr. Beasley, give this boy a job."

Mr. Beasley said, "What can he do, Mr. Rothchild?" Mr. Rothchild turned to me and asked, "What can you do?"

While for some unknown reason I was trying to stand at attention, I replied, "Anything he asks me to do, sir." Mr. Rothchild turned to Mr. Beasley. "Anything you ask him to do. When do you want him to report to work?" Mr. Beasley mumbled, "Report to me at 8:00 a.m. tomorrow."

Mr. Rothchild, who owned the company, was in town just for that day. He lived in Kansas City. After Mr. Beasley had told me to report to work the next day, Mr. Rothchild turned to me and said, "Come with me, son."

He walked me into the elevator, outside and across the street to a Coney Island hot dog stand. He ordered and paid for two hot dogs and a large glass of orange juice and commanded me to eat while we talked about my future.

You might call that luck. I don't.

I wanted to work for that company. I was going to work for that company. I went to work for that company. I never even considered another one. Think about, please, the order of things. I bathed and dressed the best I could, even though it wasn't much for getting a job at the finest clothing store in town. I groomed myself carefully. I made arrangements to work whatever hours I would be asked to work. I arrived early. I sat for eight straight hours with my hands folded in my lap. I didn't quit. And had they asked me to leave when they locked up that night I would have been there the next morning and the next until I got the job. Yes, it was lucky for me that Mr. Rothchild happened to be in Oklahoma City that day, but I would have been sitting there every day until he did come, if that's what it took. I knew in my mind that I wasn't going to quit until I got the job.

I got the job. You can, too.

45

WHAT ABOUT MANAGEMENT?

When I'm talking about opportunity for the retail salesperson who succeeds by developing into a professional selling machine, I hesitate to talk about management opportunities.

My experience has been that most mid-management retail executives are even less professionally qualified for their jobs than the average retail salesperson.

Every element of retailing is selling. *You don't get promoted out of selling!* You only move to a higher level of selling.

Don't ever think otherwise.

Advertising. Pure selling at its most sophisticated. Opportunity is unlimited for the producer of ads that sell.

Buying. If I had one dollar for every incompetent salesperson in this world who wants to be a buyer I would have tens of millions of dollars. The plague of the retail industry is the incompetents who think their job is to buy, feeling no responsibility for the selling of what they have bought. Is there opportunity in buying? Beyond your wildest imaginings for those who first master the profession of selling and then have those unique talents to take on the additional responsibility of *buying* to *sell.*

Sales Managing. For those who have truly mastered the profession of selling and are producing all of the sales they personally can produce but are driven to want to sell even more, then the only way up is to start getting other people to sell for them. Call it what you want. That's sales management. Recently, I asked a sales manager what his job was. He said, "Seeing that I have enough people scheduled and that they are following the rules." That is bookkeeping and police work, not sales management. Of course, the world of retailing is crying for those who can develop and manage professional sales organizations at high levels of production. You can write your own ticket if you can get the job done. But it "ain't easy."

Store Managing. I am always amazed at what people will do to become a store manager. They'll work around the clock. Do anything to make a sale — clean, sweep, deliver, display, load, unload, even clean the restrooms, and do windows — all to achieve that ultimate goal, the job of store manager. And then, they sit back, put their feet on the desk and violate every principle of management. Most people see management as reaching a point where they do nothing because now they can tell everyone else what to do, so they can go play golf.

If you are looking for easier work and more money, improve your selling skills. Don't choose management. What you should expect when you become a manager is more work and more responsibility. Management has its rewards in direct proportion to the added responsibility and the success you bring to your company.

Owning the company. Some see this as being your own boss. When you are a professional salesperson producing at a high rate of sales, you are already as close to being your own boss as you will ever be.

Owning your own company is a different story. At no time in history has it been easier to own your own retail company than it is now in the United States. You can acquire something to sell with little or no capital and that's all it takes to be a retailer.

Did you notice? I said "sell?"

What an opportunity.

46

THE WINNER'S
CHALLENGE

Joe Louis, the man I will always believe was the greatest prize fighter of all time, never gave up. I can remember him when I was a small child because my father was an avid fight fan. Every time Joe Louis fought, the family gathered around the radio. I still recall the announcer's voice so many times, round after round, saying how badly the opponent was beating the mighty Brown Bomber. Yet somehow, when defeat seemed inevitable, Joe Louis reached deep into his soul and won a mighty victory. I think he was the greatest and the most exciting because he had the attitude of a winner.

I will never forget the final round of the Oklahoma City Open in 1957 when Arnold Palmer was trailing by seven. I was in his army and followed him the full 18 holes. He was the only golfer exciting enough to watch all the way. You could just feel the electricity around him. When he stepped onto one elevated tee with a 420-yard dog leg, heavy trees and out of bounds to the right and a 270-yard carry over the dog leg, I said to my friend, "My God, he's lining up to carry the dog leg." He said, "No, he can't." "He is." And he did, his ball coming to rest on the fringe of the green. The most exciting golf shot I have ever seen. Even though Arnie still trailed by several strokes and was quickly running out of holes, you knew he was going to win. And he did.

All great victories go to the one who never gives up, who keeps trying when all around him have quit.

I recently went through the greatest trial of my life when my company found itself with a severe cash flow problem that very nearly destroyed it. There were hundreds of times when, all around me, the advice was: "Give it up, it's not worth the agony. Let them have it. You don't need it." All I could think of was that somehow, some way, I was going to save it. Even if I had nothing left but a door knob in my hand.

When I told my friends in and out of the industry of my intentions, that the company's problems were solely my fault, and it was my responsibility to solve them, the support came from everyone who was important. First, a personal friend came to me and said, "If you don't want to lose your company, you don't have to if you remember you have a friend." His financial help was important, but without his belief in me it was meaningless.

Then my biggest suppliers got behind me and persuaded others to support me. And those employees who were so necessary to our recovery plan gave unselfishly of themselves. The company was saved because of the support and efforts of hundreds and hundreds of people to whom I shall be forever grateful.

But the key was up to me. My friend said, "If you need money and want to save your company, I will help, but if you don't feel you can save it or don't want to, tell me how much you need and you can have it to do something else instead."

I had to decide first that I wanted to save the company and was willing to risk everything I had. After that, the most exciting things began to happen. The important people began to believe in me and support me — just like Arnold Palmer when he lined up to carry that dog leg. My most trying hours became my greatest victory.

Yes, to the victor goes the spoils. To only 25% of all salespeople goes 75% of the income. What an exciting company of people to be numbered among.

Learn what you have to learn. Practice what you have to practice until it becomes a part of you.

You need the support of all whose approval is important to you. Get your supporters to refuse to let you give up when the going gets tough. Your spouse and children or parents must support and encourage you in your hour of need. Your other outside motivation should come from your determination to prove to all those who say you can't do it that you can.

Don't give up and victory is assured. And the closer you get, the greater the crowds of supporters who'll line up to be part of your victory. Those crowds that were called Arnie's Army on the golf course will be called customers by you. Just like Arnie's followers, they will support you by the thousands wherever you go and their excitement will cause more to follow.

To all of you who were taught by this book, but more important, who applied what you learned in your own way, please write and let me know about your success. That is my ultimate reward for this exciting work.

Learn. Practice. Work.
Success is your reward.

47

GUARANTEE YOUR SUCCESS

How many hours a day or week should you work?

All the successful persons I have known started their careers by working long hours. When you start your first job, you really have two jobs. The most important as far as your career is concerned is to learn what you have to know to assure success. While you are learning and gaining experience, you must sell enough to keep the job. Any way you look at it, you are going to have to put in some long hours.

When I took my first sales job, I had a steady job in a furniture factory and a part-time job that gave me a fair income. I explained to my wife that I was going to take the sales job with no guarantee. I explained that if she would agree to this I would work so hard that within six months I would be making twice as much as I was at the time with two jobs.

I took the job and in 90 days I was better than doubling my previous income.

But, during that 90 days, nobody in that company came earlier, stayed later or worked harder than I.

After almost 40 years of owning and managing companies, I can guarantee the success of anyone, even an illiterate, who will do three things.

My dad told me as a small boy, "Son, when you get a job, always be the first one there every day. Always be the last to leave. Watch the other employees and see who works the hardest. Then, be sure that you are working harder than he is at all times, and you will never have to worry about your job or your success." Those words were spoken during the Great Depression when there were no jobs. Even then, anyone willing to follow that advice did not have to worry about working.

One of the best books I have read on selling is *How to Make Big Money Selling* by Joe Gandolfo. His product is insurance and he has become the greatest insurance salesman in history.

The only problem I find with Joe's book is that most of its readers will say, "It's fine for Joe Gandolfo to work harder than any man in insurance, but I don't want to work that hard." Those of you who read his book (and I consider it a must) please note that today he is starting to take some time to enjoy the success he has earned.

My recommendation is three-fold for the beginner or for salespeople who have jobs now but realize they don't have the knowledge and techniques to succeed.

First, determine whether you want a successful career in sales. Discuss it with your family or anyone else who might be affected by your decision. If you are engaged to be married, this is going to have a radical effect on your social life. You must have the support and encouragement and understanding of all those who are important to you.

Second, you must make a six-month commitment. Your every waking hour for six months will be dedicated to your career. Your day will begin by reading books on selling, listening to sales tapes and discussing selling positively at the breakfast table. You must read all ads in the paper about your product (skip the rest of the paper — you don't have time to waste). No television, radio or stereo for six months. If you have time to be listening, make it sales or motivational tapes.

Third, outline your plan to get the five groups of knowledge that you must have. *Stick to that plan.* Get those five groups of knowledge in 90 days *no matter how many hours or days a week it takes!*

During your working hours, concentrate on selling. Take every opportunity to talk to customers, trying to wind up with a sale every time. If it is hard for you to talk to strangers, take a Dale Carnegie course. Most people should take a public speaking course anyway.

If you have discussions, be sure they are productive. Discuss techniques and how to make them work better, not whether they work or don't work.

All the techniques taught in this book work. It is up to you to make them work for you.

Discuss your products, your company's policies, finance plans, service, delivery and advertising — always with a positive objective.

Reread this book from cover to cover *three* times underlining, important points in a different color each time. Listen to our tapes to reinforce what you read. Don't let a day go by without listening to the tapes of our seminars. If there is a seminar in your area, attend it.

This six-month commitment will change your life. At the end of six months you will have achieved a solid basis for a career that will guarantee your success for the rest of your life. You will have achieved an income level that you never dreamed possible.

Here's the bonus for this six-month commitment. You cannot totally dedicate yourself to this program for six months without an offer of management. Whether you want management or a professional sales career will be a choice you must make. You will be able to decide at the end of six months how many hours you want to work. If family, church or recreational activities are important to you, you will want to decide how much time to spend on those activities, because (and here's the exciting part) you will have the money to do those things!

A better home? Better education for your children? A new car? A boat? Membership in a country club? Isn't it exciting just to imagine this happening to you? Make this six-month total commitment to your career, follow the plan to the letter and set your goals. You cannot in your wildest dreams imagine all the good things that are going to happen in your life.

and a waste of time. Isn't it just as stupid to do *anything* that's going to increase your chances of losing a sale or of making it harder to get? This insight is one of the things that separates losers from winners in selling.

Remember what you did during the qualifying phase? If a customer asked for a specific item, you replied "Do you mind if I ask why you wanted that specific item?" You continued to qualify, in spite of the customer's specific request. You saw the logic behind that and learned what the results could be. (If you don't recall the process, go back and study that part of the qualifying phase before proceeding.)

The cold hard fact is you cannot skip the qualifying phase of the sale . . . even if you're selling a loss-leader item.

One after the other, winners told me that they never, never, never take a customer who calls for a specific item directly to it. They didn't know why, but they did know that when they did, the customer was going to be tough and maybe even impossible to sell. When they consistently followed their plan for qualifying and selection, it took them less time to make the sale.

So far, we've used a sofa for an example, but as you can see, literally any product can be substituted. With this technique, you'll make a lot more sales per customer. And, you're going to make sales a lot faster, which will give you more time to wait on more customers.

Sound exciting? You bet!

THE FINAL SELECTION SECRET

Let's all stand up and repeat aloud: Selling is a learned profession and those who become masters do so because they study and practice techniques that work.

Furthermore, the real secret to sales greatness, the one that all master salespeople keep in reserve, is that those special techniques have a back-up system. If the greeting, "May I direct you to something?" didn't get communication underway, there's a follow-up ready and another one after that until communication is established. And so it goes with *every* phase of your sales education.

The more you perfect your selection techniques, the more customers you will sell, but what about the customer who, for one reason or another, will not accept or buy the item you have selected?

Easy. While you are deciding which item will be best for your customer, you're also thinking about what the second-best might be. (Only losers wait to do this until the customer has turned down the first choice.)

> **The professional stays in command and in positive communication because he has planned his sale ahead, and he never quits at the first objection.**

When you lead you customer to the solution you have chosen, let the customer speak first. Here is where many weak salespersons make a fatal error. Most of the time, the customer will like your selection, but occasionally, you'll have a customer that takes one look and says, "Oh, I don't like this at all!"

Then where are you? Refresh your memory; reread Revelation Number 11: Old Ugly Was a Dog.

The professional doesn't blink an eye as he moves on to selection number two to make his sale. Rarely does he have to go further.

And another tip to remember throughout the selection process:

> **No professional salesperson ever knocks another product. Not his, not his competitor's. All products are good, it's just that the item he is presenting to his customer is the best for that customer.**

> **A professional salesperson doesn't have bad competitors. His competitors' companies are good. It is just that his own company is so much better.**

Finally, it is not how many times you failed that causes your ultimate failure, it is how many times you didn't try.

Do yourself this favor: Go for 100% qualification 100% of the time and you will die a respected, rich professional salesperson.

Go back over the selection technique. If it is followed religiously, it still will lead you to product selection. Do not abandon this technique *for any reason.*

As you become really familiar with and learn to rely upon your techniques, you will realize that when you practice with total effort on each one every time, even though they might work perfectly only occasionally, their combined strength will still lead you to the sale most of the time.

Here's the kicker:

> To make a sale, positive communication must be established, customer need must be determined, the product must be selected, the presentation must be made, and the sale must be closed. And this process happens when the benefits promised have assured the buyers that their buying decision will gain the approval of all those whose approval is important to them.
>
> Your selling job is made harder to the extent that you fail to fully execute any or all of the selling phases. Even with partial execution of all six, the sale can still be made almost every time. But the only way you get partial execution is by trying for complete execution. Miss or ignore any phase of the sale and the chances of losing it jump to near 75%.

27

Phase Three: Selecting

THE MONEY FACTOR

Your qualifying questions should give you enough information to determine the best solution for the customer's problem. But this decision on your part is never made with an eye toward selling your most expensive item. The items that will work best for your customers, will provide what they need — those are the items you select. But cost is a part of that decision.

After all, if you have determined that your customers are on a limited budget, the item that's best for them will be one they can afford. Pushy order takers never consider what the customers can afford and often try to sell a customer something too expensive because they will make a greater commission that way.

Professional salespeople know they are responsible for prescribing the right product at the right price and they are prepared to do so with confidence.

Here's how the professional might pose the price question: "Most people who buy better desks are prepared to spend around $500 so that's where we have our best selection, although some of our customers to whom price is not as important might spend as much as $1,000 or more and we have some desks at those prices too. Of course, we have desks for our customers on restricted budgets who can spend only around $299. Which price do you think best suits you?"

This multi-choice question always gets an answer. When you have properly structured the prices, the customer lets you know exactly where you will stand when you get to the close.

If the customers choose the $1,000 or above price bracket then you have ruled out price as a factor. All you have to do is select a desk they like and sell it. If they choose the $500 bracket and find the desk that best meets their needs at $400, they are still left with $100 they were prepared to spend and you can help them spend it on the right desk chair, can't you?

If the customers choose the $299 figure and the desk that will best meet their needs costs $400, then you know you will have to overcome a price objection. Later in the book I will give you techniques to address that objection if it has not already been overcome after your presentation of features and benefits.

Your rule of thumb on price is to set the center price — the one you want the customers to select — about 20% above the price of the item you have selected for them. The higher price should be 50% to 100% above (or simply the highest-priced items of that category your company carries). And set the lower price about 40% under your selected price.

In retail selling, other factors can come into play and cause us to recommend price selection even before you take the customer to the product.

On a retail floor, your merchandise is tagged with a price. Usually the price tag is highly visible. When you get to the item you have selected, the customer will see it as just an item and won't see all its features and benefits because you have yet to present them. Therefore, when they spot the price, it will be too high. *The customers will say, "Oh, we didn't want to spend that much," and the order taker will believe them.*

But the customers never mean they didn't want to spend that much. *They mean only that they are not going to pay your asking price for an item when its perceived value to them is probably only one-half of your sale price or even less.*

> If you establish what the customers are ready to pay as being above the price of the item you have selected for them before you show them that item, price is neutralized and doesn't become a barrier to your sale. Of course, if they were responding to an advertised time, price has already been established and accepted, provided the item met the other criteria needed to make the sale.

When you fully understand this technique, you are on your way to the top.

WHAT ABOUT SALE PRICES?

Weak salespeople never cease to amaze me on this point. For example: A company advertises a $499 gidget on sale for $299. A customer comes in and says, "I want to see those $299 gidgets you advertised today." The order taker invariably responds "Right this way!"

Top salespeople make very, very sure to do two things when selling sale-priced merchandise. Number one, they must establish the original price and value of the product firmly in the customer's mind before they ever get to the product, so when they get to the product and start their presentation, all they do is present features and benefits to establish the $499 price. They must never forget the customer came to buy a $499 gidget and that the only reason he came was because it was on sale for $299.

I mentioned that they never forget two things about sale prices. Number two is this: They must remember to make the price reduction seem reasonable to the customer. Nobody sells $100 bills for $50 unless the $100s are counterfeit.

Why do you suppose that on a day when dozens of ads appear in the newspaper proclaiming "SAVE 50% TO 75%!" No great crowds appear at the stores running the ads? After all, if you were selling dollar bills for 25 or 50 cents apiece, you'd have a riot. Yet, on that same day, a giant company, that only a few days before made front page news when a fire destroyed part of its warehouse, runs a "fire sale" ad with prices reduced up to 50%. That's the store where you'll find a mile-long traffic jam. Why? They have a reason for their sale — one that people believe. If they're going at half-price, they'll expect a little smoke damage, soil or something.

Most weak salespeople avoid the reason for a sale. A customer might be looking at a floor sample dining room suite, originally $2,000, reduced to $1,500. The customer points out a small scratch. Weak one says, "Oh! You won't get this one. You will get a brand new one from the warehouse." He just gave up his reason why the customer could save $500.

> Your techniques for making the sale remain constant.
>
> If a product isn't the best solution to the customer's problem, putting it on sale won't change that.

> If your presentation doesn't establish value at the
> level of the original price, then the sale price has no
> meaning. If there's no sound reason for the sale
> price, the customer will doubt you. People do not
> buy from someone they don't trust.

Years ago, I bought out a large furniture company at a substantial discount on their inventory. After the sale had been running for about three weeks, I was getting down to the dregs. I needed to reach a different kind of customer to sell off the balance of the inventory. I'll never forget one of the TV commercials I ran:

"When I tell you that some of our odds and ends are reduced 90%, you find that hard to believe, don't you? What if I told you we still have 88 odd dining room tables that were from $200 to $350 apiece and I would sell them to you for $8.88 each? You wouldn't believe me, would you? But I do have 88 tables and I will sell them for $8.88 each. Here's why. The tables were out of the cartons and stacked in the warehouse of the company which we bought out. If any were current models or if we had chairs and chinas to match, the price for the tables would be $200 to $350 apiece. But as a matter of fact, we don't even have the legs for these tables, so we will sell them for $8.88. We only have 88 of these but there are hundreds of similar items at similar prices at this sale."

A few minutes after opening the next morning, the table tops were sold and by the time we closed late that night, most of the inventory was sold and gone, too.

You must have a good reason for a sale price. Professionals tell the reason and in the buying fever that creates, they make lots of sales.

Remember, you are in control. You will lead your customer to the right buying decision in the shortest amount of time.

This price and selection technique works — even when customers know the technique themselves, it works. Practice it until it becomes as natural as breathing.

> While you are getting your five groups of knowledge
> and preparing yourself to sell, that is not selling.
>
> When you are greeting the customer to establish
> communication, it is not selling.

When you qualify the customer to determine his need as thoroughly as possible, that is not selling.

After you know what the customer needs and you decide on the best solution, that is not selling.

It is all just "getting ready to sell."

Until now, you have been getting prepared to make the sale. The better, more thorough job you do to get ready the easier your job of selling will be.

Remember, a surgeon's entire medical education sometimes takes 15 years or more just to get him ready to operate. Even his diagnosis of the patient is preparation. Pre-operative procedures get the patient ready for surgery. Scrub-up, gloves, and gown are all part of the preliminaries. The anesthetic is preparation, too. But until every step is completed, there will be *no* surgery.

Not yet.

The moment of truth in the life of the surgeon is when the cutting starts. So it is with selling. Infinite preparation is the mark of the professional, and until every detail is completed down to the last minute, it is still . . .

48

YOU HAVE TO HAVE GOALS

I have interviewed salespeople from 22 to 63, with from six months' to 35 years' experience. About half were men and half women.

I have interviewed salespeople working on the same sales floor. Each worked the same hours. Each had the same number of ups (or customers). Each was selling the same products with the same delivery, the same service, the same terms, the same advertising and the same inventory.

These salespeople for the most part had several years' experience in furniture sales. Those at the bottom over the last five years have averaged $15,000 to $20,000 a year. Those at the top over the same period averaged $40,000 to $100,000 a year.

Those at the bottom had few if any techniques. Without exception.

They had no practiced technique for greeting the customer. And without exception they had no technique for determining the customer's need or the related problems that is called qualifying. At the bottom, few even knew what the term meant. At best, they thought it meant finding out how much the customers could afford to spend or how big a payment they could afford. Those at the bottom could only follow the customers around until they settled on something they liked on their own. The weakest ones just stood there until the customer asked for information. At no time did they take the initiative in recommending an ideal solution to a customer's need. (Primarily because at no time, even if they took an order, did they ever have the slightest idea what the customer's need *was*.)

When asked how they translated features into customer benefits, they showed absolutely no comprehension of the subject at all. When they talked of a product feature, they in no way at any time related that to what it would or could do for the customer.

Weak ones deluded themselves into believing that they were nice people, that their customers liked them, that they weren't pushy, that from 25% to 75% of their sales were made to be-back customers.

(Be-backs are customers who come in, shop, and leave, returning later to buy the item they looked at. They are not to be confused with call customers who have bought once or more from a salesperson and call for that salesperson when they come back to make additional purchases.)

Those at the bottom had little or no call-customer following.

Those at the bottom had absolutely no closing techniques, and for the most part, never actually asked for the order.

They had never read a book on selling.

They had never listened to sales tapes.

They had never attended a sales seminar — even passing up those paid for by their company.

They all believed they could never be like those at the top, and yet most had as good or better personalities and some actually had higher I.Q.s than those at the top.

Those at the bottom had no goals. At best, their goals were to do as good a job as they knew how. (For which they had no plan at all.)

When I asked them where they were going with their career, it was as if I had asked them where they were going on a trip.

"New York City," they said.

"How are you going to get there?"

"Best way I can," they said.

"Do you have a map?"

"No."

"Which direction are you going to go?"

"Don't know," they said.

In-depth questioning revealed there was complete agreement among those at the bottom on most of the company's weaknesses. They obviously discussed every negative that arose on the sales floor because they all enumerated the same ones.

Tragically, many were young, beautiful, healthy, intelligent people, while others were past the prime of life. One man well into his 50s said he had never been very successful at anything but that he loved selling and his goal was to continue selling right up until the day he died. But with each year, his strength and sales weaken and because he has in 35 years never read a book on selling, never developed any technique for selling, his days on a sales floor are limited. The tragedy to me was the clear vision I had of the wasted, unsuccessful lives of those other still young, still beautiful, still healthy and intelligent salespeople who had the same lack of goals. They were like ships without rudders and soon they would be old.

I desperately wanted to find some way to show them how exciting and rewarding their careers could be, but I was there only to ask questions, not to teach.

In a recent interview, a salesman let me know immediately that his faith was the most important thing in his life. And all else was only temporary as he was awaiting his final reward. He said he had averaged $50,000 a year for the last five years, and he intended to continue at that level until The Rapture. He said he was a very devout Christian and he made no effort to improve his skills. He relied entirely upon his faith and motivational tapes.

Later in the interview I asked if he felt he was growing spiritually and he said yes. I asked if he thought that was necessary and he said yes. I said, "If you stop growing spiritually, you start dying spiritually." He agreed. I asked if you must grow mentally to grow spiritually and he said yes.

I said, "In 1979 you made $50,000 and in 1983 you made $50,000. Based on the compound rate of inflation, the $50,000 you made in 1983 will buy only $28,000 worth of what $50,000 in 1979 would buy." "You have stopped growing in your profession," I told him, "and I can assure you that every time you die a little in your profession, you will die a little in your faith. You have one heart, one mind, one body, and one soul. They are all either healthy, strong, and growing daily, or they are weak, sick and dying daily. They all live or die together."

Yes, you have to have goals for your life, but those goals must include every day of your life. A goal for the next life is a copout if it permits you to escape any responsibility for this life.

If there is life after death, the recorded scriptures — Christian, Jewish, Moslem, Hindu, or any of the thousands that promise on-going existence — one and all determine the rewards of that existence by what we have done in this life.

One last thing: those promised eternal rewards are based on the little things of this life, day by day. "When you have done it unto even the least of these my brethren, ye have done it unto me," Jesus said. "He who would be the greatest amongst you must first become the least."

One young man I interviewed at the top was 29 years old and his earnings already approached $100,000 a year. He reads sales books, attends seminars, listens to tapes, and is constantly growing in his profession.

He has developed excellent qualifying, selecting, presenting and closing skills. This young man has goals, both daily and long-term. I predict his personal sales will exceed $2 million a year very soon and his income will go up 30% and more because of those goals. He works four days a week on the same floor during the same hours with salespeople earning $20,000 to $25,000 a year. He is excited about what he does and he enjoys his work. For him it's easy work. For those in the $20,000 to $25,000 income bracket, it's unbearably hard and humiliating work.

One fact stands out crystal clear: nothing in this world is static. You are either growing or dying.

You can't stand still, and if there is one thing we know in this computerized, televised, space-age world, it is that you either grow faster to keep up or you die faster.

Children of the '60s were exposed through television to more things of this world by the time they were five years old than their great, great grandparents would have seen in a hundred of their lifetimes.

Many men and women throughout history who have achieved greatness in their lifetime had only normal I.Q.s.

Copernicus, credited with being the founder of modern astronomy, had an I.Q. projected at 105.

Cervantes, one of the classic writers in Spanish literature, also had an I.Q. projected at 105.

Rembrandt's I.Q. was projected at 110.

George Washington and Abraham Lincoln had I.Q.s projected at 125 and I might include Adolph Hitler at 125.

The average I.Q. is 100. It was not the great intellectual capacity of those men that was the basis for their success. It was the goals they set for themselves and their desire to achieve those goals that led to their success.

You must have goals.

When they added a reasonable amount of their five groups of knowledge, the sale was a cinch for each and every one of them. There were no longer any weak salespeople among them when they all performed these basics of selling.

Because of this episode and hundreds of similar experiences I have observed, I am convinced beyond a shadow of a doubt that most people can become high-volume, high-income retail salespeople. Every time I witness this happening and have been a part of it, it is one of the greatest joys of my life.

So read this book three times, cover to cover, underlining it each time in a different color highlighter.

Put every one of its teachings into practice.

Set your goals. You, yes *you,* are headed for the top while you enjoy the excitement and fun of the easiest high-paid work there is:

SELLING RETAIL.

have described them to you. When he finished, I asked if he leads the customer past two or more less desirable items on the way to the item that he has selected for the customer. He gave my question some thought, then answered yes. "Every time?" I asked. "Except when the store is overrun with customers. Then I might lead them directly to the item." I sat silently looking at him while he pondered what he had just said. There was an awkward silence I broke by saying, "It seems to me that the purpose of the technique is to make the sale easier, therefore faster. Wouldn't the most important time to stick to the technique be when you want to sell as fast as possible?" There was another pause. His face began to get a little red as he replied, "You know, I just can't believe that I haven't seen that myself. As I look back, I see that every time I get in a hurry and try to bypass that phase of the selection, it actually takes longer. Why, I even lost some of the sales!" This master salesperson will earn more money this year because he won't overlook that important step again.

▶ *3. This technique will not come naturally to you.* To learn it and to make it work, you will have to labor over it until it does come naturally in the course of every sale. How will you know when you have achieved the perfection of these selection techniques? The losers in the lounge will be saying, "Sure, he's a top salesperson, but that's because he's a natural — and besides, he's lucky."

When I asked the losers if they were able to learn anything from top salespeople, their answers usually implied that they believed top salespeople were born with all those techniques. By now, though, you know better, don't you?

THE CUSTOMER WHO ASKS FOR A SPECIFIC ITEM BY NAME, BRAND OR NUMBER

"Harder to sell," was the consensus of the weak salespeople, "and more often than not, the customer didn't buy it when I took them straight to it!"

The top salespeople said the same thing. Except they did not take the customer straight to the item requested, because they had learned that going straight to the item lost the sale, or at least make it harder to get.

▶ By now, I'm sure you agree that to ask "Can I help you?" is stupid

A professional who has prepared the customer mentally to spend $599 for a sofa encounters no price resistance when he recommends a sofa she can buy for $499. The customer is not on the defensive. On the contrary, she hopes that this is THE sofa and that it will do everything she needs and wants it to do.

The professional has even mentally prepared her to believe this $499 sofa is the one she likes best of all the ones she has seen. He accomplishes this by leading her to at least two other sofas that he knows will be less desirable before showing her the $499 one he has selected.

Caution: When you stop in front on one of the less desirable sofas, ◀ your comment must be non-committal. "Mrs. Jones, this is not the sofa I had in mind for you, but I wanted you to see it, just in case." And, unless Mrs. Jones goes crazy over the sofa, lead her quickly to your second "sofa stop."

"Mrs. Jones, here's another sofa I wanted you to see before I show you the one I feel best meets your needs." If Mrs. Jones stops at any other sofa along the way, let her react first, then move her to THE ◀ sofa.

Here is what happens during this process: The sofa you are leading her to is the right style, the right size, the right color, the right cover, and the price is one hundred dollars less than she was expecting to pay. The sofas you showed her on the way to THE sofa ◀ might be more or less expensive, but you know that by comparison she will like the one you have selected much better than any she has seen. The biggest surprise of all? That $100 less than she was prepared to pay.

SEVERAL POINTS FOR YOU TO REMEMBER

1. *No one is born knowing this technique.* Every top salesperson had to learn it and then perfect it through constant practice. You can learn it, too, but not without practice.

2. *You may think this technique will take too much time.* You're probably saying to yourself right now that there has to be a quicker way to make a sale.

Let me reassure you. Recently, I interviewed a retail furniture salesperson who earned over $70,000 last year. During the interview, he described his qualifying and selection phases exactly as I furniture as the sales leaders all of a sudden become every bit as good and as effective as the leaders?

The answer is so simple.

1. They believed the customer would be better off if they were getting the benefits of the product.
2. They believed the customer would buy the fabric treatment if the benefits were demonstrated to them.
3. They were knowledgeable about the product (although much of that knowledge was incorrect).
4. The customers' problem and need had been clearly determined. That is, once having bought brand new furniture they wanted to keep it looking new as long as possible. They would buy the fabric treatment for the same reason people buy seat covers for a brand new car.
5. When the weak salespeople made a dramatic demonstration of the benefits, about 80% of the customers said, "I will take it." Little or no closing effort was required on the part of the salesperson.

Every one of those weak salespeople proved:

When positive communications are established (That's the greeting technique that can be learned) —

When the customers' problem had been clearly defined (That's the qualifying technique that can be learned) —

When they could lead the customer to the best solution for the customers' need (That's the selection technique that can be learned) —

When they could make a dramatic demonstration of a product which otherwise the customer could not see, smell, taste, hear, or feel (That's the demonstration technique which can be learned) —

49

THE PROFESSION IS LEARNED

D o you remember the story about soil repellent fabric treatments in the revelation on "Benefits"? Here is another case of the 9-Dot Puzzle helping you understand the most significant lesson to be learned from this story.

You have already seen how everyone got concerned about the dealers who were selling the in-store fabric treatment. You also saw that at no time did the dealers look at what they themselves were doing — selling the fabric treatment that was already on their in-stock furniture such as ScotchGard® or Teflon®.

This is a very important lesson for all salespeople because it points out a major psychological problem. All too often, salespeople get "psyched out" by someone else's success or by what someone else is doing instead of paying attention to what *they* are doing.

Even so, this is not the ultimate lesson to be learned here.

Here is the most incredible part of this entire episode and the entire industry missed it!

> **The percentage of sales of the fabric treatment in** ◀
> **some cases was just as high by the weak salespeople**
> **as it was by the strong salespeople, even though the**
> **weak salespeople continued to sell only one-third to**
> **one-half as much upholstered furniture as did the**
> **strong salespeople.**

BUT—once either the weak or the strong had made an uphol- ◀
stered sale, the weak often sold the fabric treatment as well as the
strong did. ◀

Here is the point. When selling this product, many of the weak salespeople were every bit as good as the strongest salespeople. *Why?*

Yes, how did salespeople who couldn't even sell one-half as much selling techniques? For that new home, new car, vacation, sales volume, management position, family, church, future?

Write it down! Break it down! Then, *determination* will make you a winner.

Divide the cost of the trip plus $1,000 spending money by that many days. Chances are, your quotient will reveal that it will take only an average of less than an extra hundred dollars in sales a day to make that goal. Tell your family, your friends, reserve your vacation time at work, because on March 1 you are going to leave on a jet plane for the trip of a lifetime."

That's setting a goal, and I will guarantee you two things you can bet on.

If she doesn't go to the travel agency, if she doesn't make that reservation, if she doesn't break it down to a daily goal, if she doesn't make a commitment by telling family and friends, on March 1 the only place she will go is to work.

But, if she does all those things, on March 1 she is going to be on her way to Europe and you can bet the farm on that.

Everyone I asked about their goals had an answer. Like the 56-year-old man who said, "I just want to sell until I die," and the lady who wanted to go to Europe, the list was endless and those who were on the bottom of the sales chart without exception either had no clearly defined goals or had absolutely no plan for achieving them. None — no, not one — had written down a single goal nor committed themselves in some way to achieving it.

Goals are the very heart and soul of living. With them, we have exciting reasons to jump out of bed every morning, because we know we are on our way.

The higher up the salespeople were, the more clearly defined their goals were. Those at the top had written plans and commitments made, dates set and not even an act of God could keep them from achieving them.

No, they weren't the best educated or the smartest.

They weren't the youngest or the oldest.

They weren't the best looking or most talented.

They weren't the owner's relatives.

They were the winners in life and they all had goals.

What are yours?

Have you written them down? Have you broken them down to months, weeks, days and hours? What is your schedule for learning what you must learn? What is your schedule for developing your

Abraham Lincoln, who in my opinion was the greatest political leader in history, never had the advantages of being taught in the great universities of the world of his day, but he had goals and determination. Most historians believe we were robbed of his true greatness by his assassination and as a result of his death, our great nation suffered its darkest hours during the recovery period when the goals and plans so vividly envisioned by Lincoln were not carried out.

Most of you reading this book no doubt have I.Q.s exceeding 100 (average) and many are in the 125 range.

These examples I've just given illustrate quite clearly that a lack of high intelligence is no excuse for failure. But a lack of goals guarantees it.

Anne Frank died at fifteen and left a diary that influenced the conscience of the world.

Thomas Chatterton died at seventeen, leaving England some of its great poetry.

Joan of Arc died at nineteen and is revered as one of the greatest women in world history.

So youth is no excuse for failure.

You must have goals.

At 82, Winston Churchill wrote a history of the English-speaking people. At 89, Arthur Rubenstein gave one of his greatest recitals in Carnegie Hall. At 100, Grandma Moses was still painting her masterpieces.

So age is no excuse for failure.

You must have goals.

Patrick Henry, Daniel Webster, Abraham Lincoln, Clarence Darrow are a few of the great lawyers in American history who never went to law school. Up until the second world war over one-half of the great American fortunes had been founded by men with less than a fourth grade education.

A lack of formal education is no excuse for failure.

You have to have goals.

> You have to have goals to achieve anything in this life, but if you are going to achieve them, you have to learn everything that might be needed or which is important to their achievement.
>
> No excuse will do. If you are not enjoying all the

things you want in this life and have no goals set to get them, then the same time next year or even ten years from now, chances are you will be no nearer to gaining them.

If you want to be a better salesperson or a better parent, to have a nicer home, a better car, more leisure time with more money to enjoy, to send your children to college — whatever it is, you must first decide what it is you want. Then you determine where you are right now and what you must do that you are not doing now, then break it down into bite-sized pieces.

Let me give you an example.

I interviewed a mother in her early 40s. She was divorced and raising a twelve- and a fourteen-year-old child by herself. When I asked if she had any goals, she replied, "Only one. I have never had a vacation and I want to go to Europe."

I asked what she was doing about it.

"Well, I made up my mind that I was going to go about a year ago," she said, "so I opened a savings account just for the trip."

"When do you plan to go?"

"Oh, I don't know," she said, "but if things go well, maybe in another year or two."

I asked, "Where did you want to go and for how long?"

"Two weeks," she replied, "and I want to go to London, Rome, and Paris."

"How would you like to go next spring, maybe in March while the rates are low?"

"Oh, I couldn't go that soon," she said. (This interview took place in July.)

I asked why.

"Well, I would never have the money by then."

Then I suggested this: "On your next day off, go to a travel agency and tell them you want to take a trip to Europe. You want to leave on March 1 and return March 15. You want a tour that will take you to London, Rome, and Paris. You want to make reservations now and you need to know how much it costs. Get all the brochures on the places you wish to visit. Ask for every brochure on those cities and hotels you wish to visit. Then go to the library and check out every book on Rome, London, and Paris. Go home, sit down, and count the number of days you will be working from now until March.

NOT YET

This is it.
It's time to begin selling.
Turn the book over
for Book Two.